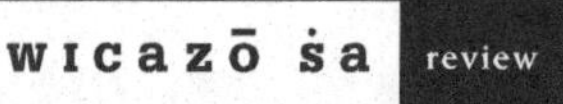

A Journal of Native American Studies

Editor
Lloyd L. Lee, University of New Mexico

Associate Editor
Amy Lonetree, University of California, Santa Cruz

Book Review Editor
Madeline Rose Mendoza, University of New Mexico

Founding Editors
Elizabeth Cook-Lynn
Roger Buffalohead
Beatrice Medicine
William Willard

Contributing Editors
Majel Boxer, Fort Lewis College
Ellen Cushman, Northeastern University
Clayton Dumont, San Francisco State University
Donald Fixico, Arizona State University
Lawrence Gross, University of Redlands
Suzan Shown Harjo, The Morning Star Institute
Sarah Hernandez, University of New Mexico
Ted Jojola, University of New Mexico
Glenabah Martinez, University of New Mexico
Cornel Pewewardy, University of Central Oklahoma
Lisa Poupart, University of Wisconsin, Green Bay
Kathryn Shanley, University of Montana
Edward Valandra, University of Manitoba
Michael Yellow Bird, University of Manitoba

Alumni Editors
Duane Champagne, University of California, Los Angeles
Steven J. Crum, University of California, Davis
Tom Holm, University of Arizona
Luci Tapahonso, University of New Mexico
Laura Tohe, Arizona State University

WICAZO SA REVIEW · SPRING & FALL 2024
VOL. 39, NOS. 1 & 2

Special Issue: Sacred Places Protection

Suzan Shown Harjo, Guest Editor

CONTENTS

Review

Editor's Commentary

Lloyd L. Lee

Yá'át'ééh! I hope everyone is doing well. Volume 39, numbers 1 and 2 (spring/fall 2024) is a combined special edition on *Sacred Places Protection.*

The special issue on *Sacred Places Protection* is introduced by Suzan Shown Harjo, who is a Cheyenne citizen and of the Cheyenne and Arapaho Tribes and Hotvlkvlke Mvskokvlke Nuyakv. The first article, by Richard W. Hill, from Tuscarora Nation, Beaver Clan, discusses what makes something sacred to Indigenous Peoples. Hill focuses on his community of the Haudenosaunee, where they acknowledge the spiritual energy that populates the landscape and how the earth has regenerative power to overcome the stains of colonization. Next, Waŋblí Wapȟáha Hokšíla (Edward Valandra, PhD), of the Sicangu Titunwan Oyate, discusses Indigenous Peoples' sacred or significant places within the context of settler colonialism, Indigenous Land Acknowledgments, and a reparative justice framework. The third piece, by the Honorable Sm3tcoom Delbert Miller of Skokomish Indian Tribe as told to and edited with Tina Kuckkahn, is a sharing of cultural knowledge handed down through generations of Skokomish peoples. Miller shares the way young people in his tribal nation were culturally trained by their elders to understand how certain places within the natural world became sacred places to Indigenous Peoples.

Implementing an autoethnographic methodology, Gabrielle Tayac, PhD, of the Piscataway Nation, interweaves memory, experience, and research to record and promote awareness of urban lands as Native and sacred lands. Her tribal nation's home lies along the Potomac River. The river is sacred in breadth and depth, and the place is spiritual as a portal to ancestors, an interrelated life source, and Piscataway people. Brett Lee Shelton, JD, from the Oceti Sakowin Oyate, summarizes the roots of US property law explaining the bundle of rights concept with respect to land. Given that the notion of rights counters many Indigenous worldviews, he explores several examples where Native Peoples could use a bundle of sticks notion to show continued relationship to, and thus continued ownership of, sacred places. Continuing in a legal vein, Tina Kuckkahn, JD, of the Lac du Flambeau Band of Lake Superior Ojibwe, describes how the federal Indian policy of assimilation led to the loss of Strawberry Island, a sacred place to both Chippewa and Dakota peoples. Kuckkahn tells the story of intensive negotiation and natural forces that helped the peoples recover Strawberry Island. In the final article, Daniel R. Wildcat, PhD, of the Yuchi/Muscogee (Creek) Nation, examines the fourth category of Vine Deloria Jr.'s four categories of sacred lands. This category of lands that Native Peoples must be ready to receive is seldom discussed; however, it is central to Deloria's corpus of work regarding American Indian religious traditions and metaphysics. Wildcat suggests Indigenous Peoples must seriously ask whether we are prepared to receive new revelations in new places in this technology-defined age. The issue closes with Stephanie Lumsden's review of *American Indians and the American Dream: Policies, Place, and Property in Minnesota* (2023) by Kasey R. Keeler.

Our next issue, volume 40, numbers 1 and 2, will celebrate the fortieth anniversary of *Wicazo Sa*, founded in 1985. We anticipate the volume will be released in late October or early November 2025, and we will host a two-day symposium on November 6 and 7, 2025, at the University of New Mexico. Please check the University of Minnesota Press website, the Department of Native American Studies website at the University of New Mexico, and *Wicazo Sa Review* social media posts (@wicazosareview) for details.

Áhéhee'! Thank you.

AUTHOR BIOGRAPHY

Lloyd L. Lee, PhD, is an enrolled citizen of the Navajo Nation. He is Kiyaa'áanii (Towering House), born for Tł'ááschíí (Red Cheeks). His maternal grandfather's clan is Áshįįhí (Salt), and his paternal grandfather's clan is Tábąąhá (Water's Edge). He is professor and chair of the Department of Native American Studies at the University of New Mexico (UNM) and editor of *Wicazo Sa Review*. His publications include *Diné Identity in a 21st-Century World* (2020) and *Diné Masculinities: Conceptualizations and Reflections* (2013), coauthor of *Native Americans and* the University of New Mexico (2017), coeditor of *The Yazzie Case: Building a Public Education System for Our Indigenous Future* (2023), and editor of three volumes: *Nihikéyah: Navajo Homeland* (2023), *Navajo Sovereignty: Understandings and Visions of the Diné People* (2017), and *Diné Perspectives: Reclaiming and Revitalizing Navajo Thought* (2014). His research focuses on Native American identity, masculinities, leadership, philosophies, and Native Nation building.

Native Sacred Places, Lifeways, and Lives Distorted in Others' Imaginings, Dogma, Language, and Law
An Introduction

Suzan Shown Harjo

In its infancy, as the victorious United States was being constituted, the official American fathers were anxious to make treaties with venerated countries for affirmation and recognition of the newly independent nation and for legitimization of its place among the world community of nations. Their models were the treaties which existed at that time between Native nations and the Dutch, British, French, Spanish, and other European peoples. However, after the Revolutionary War (or the War Between the Brothers, as some Native Peoples called it), none of the European countries would recognize or treat with the fledgling United States, for fear of Great Britain's retribution. Only the kingdom of Morocco, in North Africa, across the Mediterranean Sea and Strait of Gibraltar from Europe, was willing to stand up to Britain and enter into a treaty with the United States.

ROOTS OF DISTORTION

President George Washington and his emissaries, often his former military attachés, reached out to the Lenape (Delaware Nation), Muscogee (Creek), Haudenosaunee (People of the Longhouse, Six Nations Iroquois Confederacy), and Three Fires Council (Neshnabek, Man Sent Down from Above) of the Anishinaabe (Ojibwe, Chippewa,

Keepers of the Medicine and Faith), and Related Odawa (Ottawa, Keepers of the Trade) and Potawatomi (Bodewadmi, Keepers of the Fire) Nations. They and others were invited to treaty talks in New York City, Philadelphia, or Washington, DC (the first, second, and third US capital cities, respectively), or to Native national locations elsewhere, such as Canandaigua in Haudenosaunee territory.

The US Founding Fathers had agreed on a government of consolidated united nations, as they and their predecessors had imagined but which was unknown as an operating model in Europe. It was in this red quarter of Mother Earth (Western Hemisphere) and Turtle Island (North America) that the Europeans and Americans observed and conducted diplomatic relations using the only working models of unions of nations they ever had experienced and seen in operation.

The United States entered into treaties with various Native nations, each recognizing the other's inherent sovereignty to make and keep binding agreements of peace and friendship, forever. In the Constitution, the federal government reserved and nationalized the right to deal with Native nations, vesting authority in Congress, rather than granting it to or sharing it with the states: "The Congress shall have Power . . . To regulate Commerce with *foreign Nations, and among the several States*, and with the *Indian Tribes*" (emphasis added to highlight federal jurisdiction regarding foreign nations and Indian tribes and over the several states). This was codified in the first federal law regarding Indian dealings, the 1790 Indian Non-Intercourse Act (or Trade and Intercourse Act), to the effect that any person's or state's Indian land or other transactions would be *void ab initio*—no good from the start—without the approval of the federal government. The federal government did not count on Georgia, Massachusetts, New York, Pennsylvania, Virginia, and other powerful colonies-turned-states ignoring or defying the treaties and national laws, and persisting in taking Native lands through their own (illegal, nonnational) "treaties." The US record of keeping its treaty promises depended on the relative strength of the national government as compared with the state governments' and populations' fervor for Indian lands, water, gold, silver, copper, and other property.

In its colonial history and first centuries—and despite its treaties with Native nations—fluctuations in federal American Indian policy and practice allowed those in official positions and those within its jurisdiction to consign Native Peoples collectively and individually to inferior status by letting their backroom, barroom, and pulpit talk spill onto pages of their formal documents. Examples include the use of such terms as *merciless savages, pagans, heathens, sq**ws,* and *r*dsk*ns.* What was meant by these pejoratives was "godless," even more than "bloodthirsty" and "inferior." They were perceived to be anti-Christian, anti-Catholic, or anti-Protestant and called *soulless, uncivilized, ruthless,* *cold-blooded*, and *wild*, just for being non-European. European countries even perceived their own people or neighbors in the same way. For example, depending on the century or ruling family in England, the rulers viewed as non-English, and therefore *savage*, certain Scots in Scotland. The same was true of the French who, depending on age and noble status, viewed certain individuals as non-French, and therefore *sauvage*—which was also their view of the English. Native Peoples and many Americans were viewed as *subhuman, inhumane*, and *barbaric*, which was different from the terms like *beastly, brutish*, or *vulgar* used to refer to other Europeans who exhibited low-class, unseemly, or embarrassing behavior considered as unacceptable in polite society.

Because of these perceptions, Native Peoples were not believed to have sacred places or land rights at all. Many Europeans and Euro-Americans accepted that Indigenous persons of this hemisphere were human and had souls, for the purpose of making choices (to give up land or gold, being the most prominent examples). For some countries and religions, or their rulers, it was a "settled question" that Natives did not have souls, personhood, or humanity for the purpose of making choices and could be treated like animals on the land. Conquistadors carrying the Requerimiento had to read it in Latin to the *indios* (the Spanish cognate for the English word *Indians*) or to "empty land," demanding recognition of Catholic superiority and the Spanish right to own land and gold. If the indios did not answer or responded with anything but acquiescence, they could be enslaved or dispatched to heaven as a soul making that choice, and the killers did not face moral peril. Those who resisted could be enslaved or sent to hell as soulless, which also absolved the killer of the killing. Taking land and other things from the indios was legal under the Catholic Church's papal bulls, which initially authorized Spain's sole colonizing rights, later authorized Spain and Portugal to divide New World colonizing.

These methods, the Doctrine of Discovery, and Manifest Destiny were based on white supremacy and the Europeans' beliefs that their superiority over non-Christians and nonwhites was God-given. At best, we were, and still are, mocked as *primitive, stoic, uneducated, dirty, lazy, stupid, useless, unworthy, worthless*, and *wooden Injuns*; as well as referred to by denigratory terms that are palmed off as honorifics: *chief, king, princess, Indian maiden, brave, shaman, ringleader, troublemaker, warrior*, and *noble savage*.

Keep in mind that this language and use of words as weapons were imposed by people who left or fled their relatives and old countries, leaving behind those who beheaded, dismembered, scalped, and skinned their own, and that some of those émigrés committed some of the same deprivations themselves. Others left behind family members whose dying or lifeless bodies lined roads and bridges to castles, churches, and royal hunting grounds or whose heads were mounted on spears or impaled on wooden stakes as a warning to would-be trespassers or violators of any of the rulers' laws. Some of them helped make the Inquisition a state sport, and they and others worked their women, children, and poor people like oxen and slaves until they dropped. European émigrés brought bubonic plague, smallpox, cholera, syphilis, and other deadly infectious diseases—along with their domesticated animals and rats and fleas that also carried diseases—and introduced into this hemisphere measles, mumps, rubella, tuberculosis, diphtheria, typhoid fever, influenza, pneumonia, the common cold, and other infections against which their populations had developed varying degrees of immunity, but which became raging epidemics among Native Peoples. Many also imported cultivated diseases of human depravity: gold fever, land lust, money hunger, and insatiable greed for silver, copper, lead (and uranium and other "energy resources" and lithium and other "green elements" today), as well as for trees, mercury, oil, water, and coal.

NAMING, RENAMING, CLAIMING, RECLAIMING

In addition to using pejoratives to subjugate Native individuals and groups, Europeans wielded language that presaged harmful actions against Native lands, waters, and land and water features, in order to separate Native Peoples from places that were essential to Native cultural, economic, social, and spiritual well-being and survival. This was the equivalent of strangers planting a flag and "discovering" others' property. The European sailors and priests in 1492 were prepared for claiming land, but not quite for the land they "discovered," which meant that they stumbled into their naming-and-claiming particulars in this hemisphere.

Christopher Columbus drifted into the Caribbean Sea, landed in the Bahamas, lurched into his "discovery of India," and called the people who fed the Spaniards "indios." Columbus (born Cristoforo Columbo, in 1451, in Genoa, Italy) was known as Cristóbal Colón in Spain, whose king and queen financed him to find a new trade route to India for their country. Another Italian explorer who sailed for both Spain and Portugal from 1497 to 1504, Amerigo Vespucci of the Republic of Florence (Americus Vespucius in Latin), claimed the southern half of the Western Hemisphere as the "New World." One of the first cartographers to map the New World, Martin Waldseemüller, thought Vespucci, and not Columbus, made the "discovery" and so named the southern part of his 1507 map "America." From those early errors have come today's thousands of places named Columbus, Columbia or Colombia, and North and South America.

In his first hours in office on Inauguration Day, January 20, 2025, President Donald J. Trump issued Executive Order 14172, Restoring Names That Honor American Greatness, unilaterally renaming the

Gulf of Mexico as the Gulf of America. The name Mexico itself comes from Mexica, the language of the Aztec Empire. In the same order, he changed Denali, the Native name of the mountain in Alaska, back to the American-imposed Mount McKinley.

In North America, traditional Indigenous names of places have been ignored and replaced with names of persons who erased the Native past:

- **Military leaders who fought or massacred Native Peoples in the vicinity.** Black Elk Peak is held sacred by the Lakota and Oce Sakowin (Great Sioux Nation), Cheyenne (Tsistsistas), and many other Native Peoples. The highest point in the He Sapa (Black Hills; "black ridge" in the Lakota language), the Black Elk Wilderness, South Dakota, and the United States east of the Rocky Mountains, it is where Black Elk, an Oglala Lakota medicine man and visionary, received a vision at age nine. That vision is the subject of John G. Neihardt's oft-reprinted book, Black Elk Speaks: Being the Life Story of a Holy Man of the Oglala Sioux (1932) and numerous subsequent analyses. In 2016, the US Board on Geographic Names voted twelve to zero (with one abstention) to rename the sacred place Black Elk Peak. This name replaced Harney Peak, its name since 1855, the year when US Army General William S. Harney's command killed half the families in the camp of Wakíŋyaŋ Čík'ala (Brule Lakota Chief Little Thunder) in the Harney Massacre (also called the Battle of Blue Water Creek). Two of the site's previous names in Lakota are Hiŋháŋ Káǧa (Owl Maker) and Heȟáka Sápa (Elk Black).

- **European or American officeholders or heroes.** Denali is the original name for the world's third most isolated and tallest mountain (Deenaalee, The High One), in the Koyukon language of the Alaska Athabaskan Dena, the People North of the Mountain. Mount McKinley was its official US name from 1917 to 2015, first dubbed so in 1896 by a gold prospector to support the campaign of William McKinley, the twenty-seventh US president (from 1897 until his assassination in 1901). In 1975, the Alaska Board on Geographic Names and the Alaska legislature voted to change the name back to Mount Denali, but the congressional delegation of Ohio (McKinley's home state) repeatedly introduced a status quo bill, meaning the

US Board on Geographic Names could not go forward because a related bill was pending. In 1980, President Jimmy Carter established the Denali National Park and Preserve, which encompassed the mountain, when he signed the Alaska National Interest Lands Conservation Act, but both sides were unhappy with this solution, and the pending-legislation game continued for more than two decades. In 2015, Interior Secretary Sally Jewell used existing legal authority to resolve the impasse by acting as the US Board on Geographic Names and decreeing that the name would be changed. President Barack Obama traveled to Alaska and announced that the mountain's name would revert to Denali. In 2025, President Trump (whose vice president hails from Ohio and whose top advisor is running for that state's governor) issued an executive order striking down the original name Denali, reimposing the name McKinley, and directing the replacement of the members of the US Board on Geographic Names within seven days.

- **Friends or relatives of the persons doing the renaming or who hiked in, swam in, or mapped the places.** Many Native Peoples in the Pacific Northwest are seeking to change the name of Mount Rainier, the tallest mountain in both Washington and the Cascade Range. An active stratovolcano with glaciers and two craters on top, the mountain is some sixty miles south-southeast of Seattle, on the edge of Puget Sound, near Tacoma and the Port of Tacoma, parts of which are within the Puyallup Tribe of Indians' reservation. The Puyallup Tribe is leading the initiative to restore the name Mount Tahoma (Mother of Waters). Among the various Native names for the mountain are xʷaq̓ʷ ("sky wiper" or "one who touches the sky") and təqʷubəʔ in the Lushootseed language (Tacoma, Tacobet, "snow-covered mountain"), and təx̣ʷúma (or təqʷúmen) and Tax̱úma in the Cowlitz and Yakama Sahaptin languages, respectively. British Royal Navy captain and explorer George Vancouver named the mountain to honor his friend, Rear Admiral Peter Rainier, who fought for the British Royal Navy in the American Revolutionary War. The US Board on Geographic Names made the name official in 1890, and President McKinley approved an 1899 congressional act establishing Mount Rainier National Park as the fifth federal park, "for the benefit and enjoyment of the people." In addition to granting the secretary of the interior authority to approve roads, bridle paths, buildings, railroads, and other businesses, the law also states, "[The secretary] shall provide against the wanton destruction of the fish and game found within said park. . . . He shall also cause all persons trespassing upon the same . . . to be removed therefrom." Far from being "trespassers," many Native Peoples live around Tahoma and have millennial and continuing relationships with her. Even more live there for certain seasons for purposes of conducting ceremonies; fishing, gathering, hunting, and trading; maintaining good health with hot springs, mineral waters, and other healing sources; and keeping the mountain healthy with such practices as crop rotation, soil enrichment with fish and water plant nutrients, and controlled burns to protect the animals and forests and to enhance the meadowlands for the birds and insects. Among those with ancestral lands and use rights are the Confederated Tribes and Bands of the Yakama Nation and the Cowlitz, Muckleshoot, Nisqually, and Puyallup Tribes.

CHANGING NAMES OF NATIVE PEOPLES AND PLACES AS A KEY TO GAINING LANDS

Colonizers, proselytizers, speculators, miners, settlers, squatters, clear-cutters, and others—secure in their delusions of racial supremacy and legal fictions of Manifest Destiny and Doctrine of Discovery—renamed and broke apart Native Peoples, territories, and places in efforts to humiliate, divide, and conquer. These tactics and goals undercut or nullified unified efforts within and across Native Nations to assert their common interests and to resist non-Native control and ownership of all that Native Peoples depend on, have millennial relationships with, and owe responsibilities to. Among these are

- lands, waters, animals, birds, water beings, plants, forests, essential elements, and minerals;
- ancestral messages etched in stone, painted on walls, carved into trees, burned and scratched on bark, enshrined along pathways, and cut into story caves and teaching stones;
- landforms, mazes, earthworks, mounds, pillars and sentinels, balancing rocks, water features, gifts of sea or sky, and effigies of animal, bird, and water spirits;

8

- viewscapes and points for watching and recording movement in the sky, for tracking and learning from stars and planets, and for making calendars of seasons, dreams, and visions; and,
- areas of sensitivity and places of origin, departure, remembrance, celebration, observance, commemoration, condolence, ceremony, gathering and making medicine, visions, renewal, transformation, approach, and marking passages of time and generations.

The following are examples of Native Peoples who experienced colonization practices of naming and claiming; that is, stripping original, self-identified names and substituting ones of enemies or colonizers, imposing "names" with insulting character traits or personae, and benefiting from destabilization and reidentification conflicts. The first example, the Lenape (Original People), is presented in some detail, in order to provide a glimpse into the innumerable changes that take place once colonization of name and place occur, and in order to provide a historical, cultural, and language-use context for the other examples of colonization naming that are little more than listings.

LENAPE (ORIGINAL PEOPLE) AND LENAPEHOKING (LAND OF THE LENAPE)

The historic Lenape (Original People) comprised three major groups—Munsee (People of the Stony Country, Wolf Clan, Tukwsit); Unami, (People Downriver, Turtle Clan, Pukuwanku); and Unalachtigo (People near the Ocean, Turkey Clan, Pele)—and the related Muh-he-con-ne-ok (Mohican, People of Waters That Are Never Still) and Munsee-speaking Wappini (Wappinger, Easterners), and other peoples. The Lenapehoking (Lenapehokink, Land of the Lenape) along the Lenapewihittuck (River of the Lenape, now known as the Delaware River), extended from the Delaware River Valley (Delaware Bay region, northern Delaware, and the northeastern tip of Maryland), north to eastern Pennsylvania and Scheyichbi (Land Between Waters, now known as New Jersey), and Manahatta (Hilly Island, now New York City); and the western Pennsylvania and eastern Ohio sides of the Ohio Valley. There, they were closely allied with the Saawanooki (Shaawana, Shawun, or Shawnee), whose territory was south of Lenape land and who called the Lenape "Grandfathers." The Mohican homelands included areas from Albany, New York, to nearby Vermont; the "praying town" of Stockbridge, Massachusetts; and the east side of the Hudson River Valley (Mahicannituck). The Wappini were in southern New York and western Connecticut.

The venerable Lenape made one of the earliest Native treaties with Europeans, the 1682 Treaty of Shackamaxon (Sakimauchheen, Place to Make a Chief), a sacred place of condolence and commemoration overlooking the Lenape River and Coaquannock (Cuwequenaku, the Grove of Long Pine Trees, now Philadelphia). Underneath the Great Elm Treaty Tree, Lenape Turtle Clan Chief Tamanend and Proprietor William Penn (English and Dutch) of the British Colony of Quakers pledged love and friendship forever. There are four known remaining wampum belts depicting the treaty, all made of purple-and-white shell beads. Two of them show two stick figures, one with a hat, standing side by side and holding hands, symbolizing a treaty of peace and friendship. Another wampum shows meandering lines, meaning the borders were fluid, the residents of the Pennsylvania Colony could live on and use the agreed-upon Lenape land, and the colonists were free to cross into Lenape territory for hunting or other needs. Still another wampum shows four simple stick-figure crosses inside four large crosses outlining them. This has been misinterpreted by some museums and collectors as the Lenape giving the colony land, rather than as a very specific peace and friendship treaty among the three Lenape clans and the Pennsylvania Colony. The crosses have a double meaning for these parties: the centrality of the crucifix in the colony's Christian religion and the importance of the Morning Star in the Lenape cosmos.

Both Tamanend and Penn were beloved figures, and the colonists established the Tamanend Society (later, Tammany Hall in New York City), whose members/orators dressed "as Indians" and delivered speeches in the treaty-making style of the Lenape and Quakers that respected silences and punctuated oratory with periods of quietude, reflection, and exchange of wampum and other gifts. The Lenape had no way of knowing that Britain's King Charles II had claimed and "owned" much of Lenape territory (now, Pennsylvania and Delaware), which Penn and King Charles interpreted as a charter to treat with the Lenape and "purchase" lands. Penn, who converted to Quakerism as a young man and desired to found a "beloved community," later changed Shackamaxon to Philadelphia, a name that combines two Greek words to mean "brotherly love." Penn later changed Lenapehoking to Sylvania (Latin for "forests") and Charles later renamed it Pennsylvania in honor of Penn's late father, an admiral and counselor to the king, and recognized the younger Penn as founder of the New World's Province of Pennsylvania.

After Penn's death in 1718, his sons engaged in a blatant land swindle known as the 1737 Walking Purchase, involving a false treaty and resulting in a land grab of 1,200 square miles of Lenape territory, the size of present-day Rhode Island and almost the size of Delaware. This displaced many Lenape families and made it difficult for them to return to some of their most important cultural, ceremonial, and historical landscapes. Some Lenape people were pushed north to Haudenosaunee lands, and many others were forced west to their Ohio Valley fishing, hunting, and sacred grounds, where they sided with the French against the British, who claimed ownership of Lenape and other Native lands and established trade routes through them.

"DELAWARE" AND THE AMERICAN VERSION OF PEACE, FRIENDSHIP, FOREVER

Along with physical displacement, the Lenape were pressured into accepting a second name, the Delaware Nation. In 1665, the British started renaming features of Lenape territory, beginning with Delaware Bay, which was renamed after Jamestown's second and Virginia Colony's first British governor, Thomas West, Baron De La Warr. The first known treaty between the new United States and a Native Nation was the September 1778 Treaty with the Delaware (Treaty of Fort Pitt), but it began to break down as the Revolutionary War continued and the Americans could not keep their treaty promises. The Lenape split into war and peace groups, most allying with the Americans, others with the British, and still others consolidating Lenape cohesion and strengthening ties with the Shawnee and other Native allies. Lenape individuals and whole families sought solace in Christian "praying towns," especially those of the Moravian Brethren. In 1782 at Gnadenhutten (now in Ohio), nearly one hundred peaceful Lenape men, women, and children, who had been converted to Christianity by Moravian missionaries, were mutilated and clubbed to death as they knelt, prayed, and sang hymns by Pennsylvania militiamen seeking revenge for an earlier Indian attack and targeting the wrong people. When word spread of the massacre of the Delaware, Munsee, and Mohican "praying Indians," their relatives and many other Lenape lost trust in the Americans. Some fled their Ohio Valley homeland, others stayed to defend it, some joined with the British and their Native allies, while others upheld their end of the treaty and fought alongside the patriots until the shooting stopped in late 1782.

The seven-year American Revolutionary War ended with the signing of the Treaty of Paris in 1783, but warfare and constant turmoil persisted for generations of Lenape and virtually all other Native Peoples in the Northeast, Ohio Valley, Great Lakes, and Southeast. The Delaware Nation and Shawnee Nation leaders upheld their treaty relationships and treaty-making with the US federal government, which was not strong enough to enforce all treaty provisions against the powerful colonies-turned-states. Many Delaware and Shawnee citizens lost heart and wanted to retaliate against non-Natives, including the US government, and did so through Tecumseh's Confederacy, led by Shawnee leader Tecumseh and his brother, Tenskwatawa (Prophet); their mother was Hotvlkvlke Mvskokvlke, Wind Clan, Muscogee Nation. Tecumseh's Confederacy was joined by half of the Muscogee Nation (called "Creeks" by the Europeans) and citizens of other nations, who were disillusioned by the persistent violations of their treaties with the United States. Tecumseh's War ended with the 1813 death of the leader, the Prophet's escape to Canada, and the burning and razing of Prophetstown, the spiritual and political center of the confederacy.

After Lenape Nation citizens fled the Ohio Valley and other Lenape lands for Canada, their Lenape descendants founded the Delaware Nation at Moraviantown, Ontario. Today, there are three nationally recognized Lenape/Delaware First Nations on two reserves near Brantford, Ontario, Canada: Munsee–Delaware Nation (previously Munsee of the Thames) near St. Thomas; Delaware Nation at Moraviantown (previously Moravian of the Thames) near Chatham-Kent; and Delaware of Six Nations (at Six Nations of the Grand River).

The Lenape, the Shawnee, and other Native Peoples who stayed in their homelands were forced from them under the Indian Removal Act. The Lenape groups were divided up and relocated in various areas by the US government as the Delaware Tribe of Indians (northeastern Oklahoma), the Delaware Nation (western Oklahoma), and the Stockbridge-Munsee Community Band of Mohican Indians (in Shwano County, Wisconsin).

ADDITIONAL NATIVE PEOPLES AND LANDS CHANGED BY COLONIZATION

The following are but a very few examples of the 574 Native Nations, Pueblos, and other peoples today that have treaties or other formal relationships with the United States, all of which have tumultuous histories of being subjected to and suffering from colonization. These examples are presented with only minimal detail, touching lightly on their cultures, histories, and languages; their traditional names for themselves and their places; changes imposed by their colonizers; and their present efforts to reclaim national, personal, and place names. Also noted are their recovery and restoration of sacred places and other historic lands that were stolen outright, were confiscated under the color of law, were designated as regions where Native Peoples could not go (or were removed from and could not reach); or were developed, razed, or otherwise rendered unrecognizable. These examples are intended to provide a glimpse into the innumerable changes that take place once colonization of name and place occur, and to provide a historical, cultural, and language-use context for the other examples of colonization naming.

Mvskokvlke (Related Peoples)

The Europeans and Americans labeled some two hundred nations, grounds, and towns of the Muscogee Confederacy as Creeks, because they lived around flowing waters. They also were called Upper and Lower Creeks, with southern states promoting an artificial "Creek civil war" to secure Muscogee lands. Eventually, the Mvskokvlke were forcibly removed (under President Andrew Jackson's Indian Removal Act of 1830) from their Southeast homelands to Indian Territory (now Oklahoma), where they were funneled into a single Muscogee (Creek) Nation on one reservation. Some Mvskokvlke Peoples have since reestablished their identities as separate tribal entities (Thlopthlocco Tribal Town, for example). During the Trails of Tears, the ceremonial fires were "carried on our backs" and the grounds were reestablished in the new lands under the same names—Hickory Ground (Oce Vpofv), for example—and in the same proximity to one another as they had been in the "old fields." Despite the trauma of removal, the penalties for breaking civilization rules, and the dangers of traveling back home, some Mvskokvlke returned periodically through hostile Alabama, in order to honor their ancestors, gather medicine, and keep ceremonial obligations.

The ancestral Hickory Ground is in Wetumpka (which means "tumbling water" in the Mvskoke language). This name refers to the Coosa River's rapids, called Devil's Staircase by the Euro-American settlers. "Coosa" is the English version of Ani'Ku'sa, the Cherokee language (Tsalagi Gawonihisdi) word for Muscogee Creek People; and Ku'sa, the Muscogee Nation's name for this waterway, which connects with the Tallapoosa to form the Alabama River. In the Choctaw (Chahta Achvffa) language, Alba-amo means "thick vegetation" and "to clear," hence "Thicket Clearers."

For nearly 175 years, Hickory Ground was protected by the removed Oce Vpofv and later by the Alabama State Historic Commission and its 1980 listing on the National Register of Historic Places. However, it fell victim to the greed of a group of former "unorganized descendants" that received tribal and federal recognition from Congress in 1984 as the Poarch Band of Creek Indians after being denied federal acknowledgment through the Executive Branch process based on the facts and their history. Irrespective of the Poarch promise to protect it, Hickory Ground was plowed under in secret sometime before 2006. Homes and human remains were pulverized, dirt was trucked off-site, concrete was poured, and a casino and parking garage were built atop the sacred and historic place. Hickory Ground was the last capital of the Muscogee Nation before its citizens were removed to Indian Territory at gun- and bayonet-point. The present-day capital is at Okmulgee, Oklahoma (okimulgi, "bubbling water" in the Hitchita "Lower Creek" language). In addition to committing des-ecration like none of the other nearly six hundred federally recognized Native Nations have ever done to build a gaming operation, the new Poarch Band in Alabama exhumed dozens of Oce Vpofv ceremonial leaders, wrapped their remains in newspapers, stuffed them in tin water pails, and stored them in a metal trailer without air-conditioning. The precious things the ancestors wore and were buried with were stashed at Auburn University, where they remain today. Poarch individu-als claim to have reburied the deceased with "ceremony," but none of the Poarch spoke Mvskoke or had traditional cultural knowledge or agency. The matter remains in litigation, with the Muscogee Nation, Hickory Ground, and the Oce Vpofv Mekko having won a favorable ruling in 2024, when the US Eleventh Circuit Court of Appeals found error in the ruling of the judge for the Middle District of Alabama District Court and remanded the case for additional consideration. In the meantime, the Muscogee Nation continues to carry out its respon-sibilities regarding its pre-removal ceremonial, burial, historical, and commemorative sites, while the Poarch Band attempts to claim areas as their own ancestral places.

Haudenosaunee (Peoples of the Longhouse)

The Haudenosaunee, or Six Nations Confederacy, comprise the Cayuga (*Gayogoho:no'*, People of the Wet Lands, Great Swamp), Mohawk (*Kanien'keha:ka*, People of the Flint, Keeper of the Eastern Door), Oneida (*Onyota'a:ka*, People of the Standing Stone), Onondaga (*Ononda'gega*, People of the Hills, Central Fire), Seneca (*Onodowaga'*, People of the Great Hill, Keeper of the Western Door), and Tuscarora (*Skarù:rę' Kayeda:kreh*, People of the Milkweed or Hemp). The French renamed the Haudenosaunee the Iroquois (from the Huron word *Irinakhoiw, meaning* "black snakes" with a French-style *-ois* ending), and the groups became separated by the imported European wars, the US–Canada border, and the conflicting policies of US states and Canadian provinces. Most of their lands were taken in illegal trans-actions by the states of New York and Pennsylvania and Americans in those jurisdictions. Their lands along the Allegheny River in Pennsylvania, which were treated for by President George Washington and set aside for Seneca Chief Cornplanter, were taken by the federal government to build the Kinzua Dam in 1960. President Washington had written a letter to the Seneca Nation, stating that the first of the Indian Trade and Intercourse Acts of 1790 meant that they were secure in their territories and never would be defrauded of their lands. As more and more Haudenosaunee territory was taken by individual, corporate, city, county, and state squatters, trespassers, thieves, and fences, the Six Nations petitioned presidents and made new treaties; objected to the breaking of new and old treaties; watched the enactment of new federal and state laws; and saw progressively more of their lands, waters, and sacred places go under non-Native control. During the latter half of the 1900s, white people were rallying against the Haudenosaunee and most other Native Nations in local, regional, and national anti-Indian/anti-treaty hate groups. One such coalition was the Interstate Council on Equal Rights, which called for abrogation of treaties and an end to Indians' "privileges and special rights." Those rights and privileges involved writing letters, petitions, and entreaties to each incoming US president and other orderly processes available to everyone. The only difference is the treaty basis for redress of stolen land and poisoned water. In 1979, the US Supreme Court ruled on Washington State's claim that Indian treaty-guaranteed fishing rights were "special rights" and thus unconstitutional. Writing for the majority, Justice John Paul Stevens wrote that treaties are valid and binding, that tribal nations exist, and that neither of these facts interferes with the constitutional rights of non-Natives. The reason no non-Indians were challenging the treaties was because they were being broken, and no one was suggesting that the cession of Native lands that benefited non-Natives should be returned in the breaking of existing treaties. New York state and local governments, and the businesses they sanctioned, have never run out of justifications for why they continue to hold, profit from, and damage Haudenosaunee lands. Some of the Six Nations tribes held ninety-nine-year leases that ran out or were close to running out, but non-Native opponents said that treaties and laws made in the meantime removed any mandate to return tangible property and that they were not responsible for the devastated lives of Haudenosaunee citizens. They also claimed to have acquired ownership of treaty and other lands and waters by virtue of their long occupation there.

For many years, it was difficult for the Haudenosaunee to take these issues to court because adversaries even claimed they lacked standing because they had ceased to exist in the 1800s. The Cayuga, Oneida, and Onondaga Nations finally were able to file separate suits for land returns under the 1790 non-intercourse law, which non-Native persons and state governments had violated by acquiring lands without federal approval. The Oneida case reached the US Supreme Court first, where Associate Justice Ruth Bader Ginsburg wrote the 2005 decision for the Court, ruling against the Oneida Nation because it waited too long before filing suit and because returning lands now would be too disruptive for the non-Native landholders. The opinion also stated that Native land was not property until it was stolen and that dispossession was legitimized by the Doctrine of Discovery, as Chief Justice John Marshall applied it to lands in the United States in 1823. The Doctrine of Discovery is cited in the decision's first footnote: "Under the 'doctrine of discovery.' . . . fee title to the lands occupied by

Indians when the colonists arrived became vested in the sovereign—first the discovering European nation and later the original States and the United States." The same reasoning was applied to the other cases, so that court victories and property were handed to the non-Natives who were benefiting from generational use of stolen lands.

In 2023, the Vatican repudiated the papal bulls on which the Doctrine of Discovery *was based*, stating:

> The legal concept of "discovery" was debated by colonial powers from the sixteenth century onward and found particular expression in the nineteenth century jurisprudence of courts in several countries, according to which the discovery of lands by settlers granted an exclusive right to extinguish, either by purchase or conquest, the title to or possession of those lands by indigenous peoples. Certain scholars have argued that the basis of the aforementioned "doctrine" is to be found in several papal documents, such as the Bulls *Dum Diversas* (1452), *Romanus Pontifex* (1455) and *Inter Caetera* (1493). . . . The "doctrine of discovery" is not part of the teaching of the Catholic Church. . . . In no uncertain terms, the Church's magisterium upholds the respect due to every human being. The Catholic Church therefore repudiates those concepts that fail to recognize the inherent human rights of indigenous peoples, including what has become known as the legal and political "doctrine of discovery."

Neither the Supreme Court nor its Catholic members have responded to the Church's statement. Justice Ginsburg did say privately to several Native people that she regretted the line of decisions based on the Doctrine of Discovery.

One of the few bright spots in legal cases involving the Haudenosaunee is the 2024 return of more than one thousand acres near Onondaga Lake, which the Onondaga call Ohneganoh (Cool Water) and which is central to the origin of the Six Nations Confederacy. For a century, from 1881 to 1986, Honeywell International, General Motors, and other entities poisoned Onondaga Lake and Creek by dumping methylmercury and other deadly chemicals into them. The State of New York sued the chemical dumpers for environmental contamination in 1989, the area was declared a federal Superfund site, and assessments of the needed cleanup started. In 2018, lawsuits valued at some $25 million in damages were settled with a consent decree involving return of the land; nineteen conservation projects, such as in-lake habitat enhancement and native grassland restoration; and a $5 million future projects fund. The one thousand acres contains two sacred places, the headwaters of Onondaga Creek, more than forty-five acres of wetlands and floodplains, and 980 acres of forests and fields in the Tully Valley, New York. The land is near the Onondaga territory and within its ancestral homelands reserved in the 1794 Treaty of Canandaigua between the Haudenosaunee and the US federal government; it is home to a variety of wildlife: bald eagles, frogs, great blue herons, hawks, songbirds, turtles, waterfowl, and white-tailed deer. This is the largest land return to a Native Nation in New York and the first land transferred directly to and under the sole ownership and stewardship of Onondaga Nation. Honeywell, the GM bankruptcy settlement, and other sources will pay for the nineteen conservation projects. The settlement lands are part of a 2.5-million-acre strip in central New York, running from Pennsylvania to Canada, that the Onondaga Nation is pursuing as having been stolen by state and private interests, in violation of treaties with the United States and of federal laws, starting in 1788. The larger case is before the Inter-American Commission on Human Rights of the Organization of American States.

Lakota, Dakota, and Nakota

The Lakota, Dakota, and Nakota (Friend, Ally) of the Oceti Sakowin Oyate (Seven Council Fires of the Great Nation) were separated into bands and tribes called Sioux (from the Odawa word Nadowessiwag, "little snakes," filtered through French as Nadouessioux) and the Great Sioux Nation. The tribal lands were divided and diminished by gold rushes, allotment policies, and non-Native development and encroachment. The sacred He Sapa (Black Hills in Lakota) was reserved in the Fort Laramie Treaty of 1868, but the federal government looked the other way as Lt. Col. George Armstrong Custer of the Seventh Cavalry spread word of a gold strike there and as the He Sapa was overrun and transfigured by prospectors, bankers, cattle and sheep ranchers, farmers, developers, and missionaries. The Great Sioux Nation has been trying to regain He Sapa for more than 150 years. In 1980, the US Supreme Court awarded the Sioux $120 million for theft of the Black Hills, stating, "A more ripe and rank case of dishonorable dealings will never, in all probability, be found in our history." The Lakota Peoples have refused to take the money—a sum that, with accrued interest, tops $2 billion today—insisting that the sacred is not for sale and the land—at least the public lands—must be returned.

In 2012, the Crow Creek, Rosebud, and Standing Rock Sioux Tribes and the Shakopee Mdewakanton Sioux Community purchased 1,900 acres of prairie grassland and pine forests for $9 million, and in 2014 purchased an additional 437-acre tract for $2 million. The lands, known as Pe Sla, were placed in trust status in 2017 and are within the Black Hills National Forest. The tribes moved buffalo to *Pe' Sla* and by 2019 had sixty-five head of buffalo on the land year-round. The Sioux tribes consider *Pe' Sla* to be their home in their creation story and central to their culture, beliefs, star knowledge, and connection to the buffalo.

Mniwakan Oyate means Spirit Lake People. Their lake was always Spirit Lake. When non-Natives came with the goal of "civilizing" Native Peoples, they changed perfectly fine names to something that condemned Native ways. Thus, Spirit Lake became Devils Lake and the people were called Devils Lake Sioux. After years of resenting the demeaning name, they finally got the Bureau of Indian Affairs to change its records and, as of 1996, they are once again the Spirit Lake Tribe.

Other Acts of Erasure

The Anishinaabe (Beings Made of Nothing; Original People) Council of Three Fires of the Odawa, Ojibwe, and Potawatomi Nations and the Algonq`uin, Mississauga, and Nipissing Peoples were lumped together as Bands and Tribes of Chippewa (Puckered Moccasin People), and they were denied access to their ceded use areas for hunting, fishing, and gathering off-reservation until the 1980s, after more than seventy-five years of litigation over their treaty rights.

Tsistsistas (Human Beings) were renamed Cheyenne (the French version of a Lakota word, Sahiyena (meaning Little Sahiya, People of a Different Speech).

Tohono O'odham (Desert People) were called Papago (Spanish word for "bean eaters") by Spanish, Mexican, and American colonizers. They reclaimed their traditional name in the 1970s and informed the US Bureau of Indian Affairs that it needed to change its paperwork to reflect their decolonization action. The BIA agent they met with replied, "What's wrong with Bean Eater? I wouldn't mind being called that." Ok, the head of the delegation responded. "You be called Bean Eater and when you write to us, write: Tohono O'odham."

Nde (The People) Te-go-suk (Place of the Yellow Water) was changed to Tonto *Apache* (*tonto* is Spanish for "stupid," and *apachu* means "enemy" in the Zuni language).

Pueblo peoples (*pueblo* is Spanish for "town") encompass nineteen settlements. The Spanish conquistadors changed most of their original names to names of Catholic saints, such as Santo Domingo (now reclaimed as Kewa in the Keres Language) and San Juan or San Juan de los Caballeros, which reverted to its original Tewa name, Ohkay Owingeh (Place of the Strong People). Other names of pueblos came from Spanish but not from saints' names, such as Cochiti (Kotyit), and some pueblos kept their original names, such as Taos (Place of Red Willows), but continue to use "Pueblo" as part of their official name.

For more than a half century, from the early 1880s to the mid-1930s, the federal Civilization Regulations were enforced against Native persons suspected and accused of violating them. Common practices in Native cultures were criminalized, and serious penalties were levied against "hostiles" at a time when being branded a "hostile" was tantamount to a death sentence and often triggered a capture-or-kill arrest order given to the cavalry or Indian police. Prominent victims of these regulations included Hunkpapa Lakota leader and visionary Sitting Bull (Tatáŋka Íyotake, Buffalo Bull Who Sits) and his half brother, Mniconjou Lakota Chief Spotted Elk (Uŋpȟáŋ Gleška), also known as Chief Big Foot.

Starvation was used tactically as a weapon of war by the exterminationists and indiscriminately as a weapon of peace by the civilizationists. Even where the Civilization rules specified a maximum length of time that one could be imprisoned or starved, the same rules put duration of punishment under the discretionary authority of the federal Indian agent. Starvation was the most severe penalty during the Civilization period, when Native Peoples were moved away or kept from traditional and cultivated foods; the buffalo were being killed off as a way of controlling or killing Indians; deer, antelope, and other animals were declining as a result of deforestation by the Euro-American settlers; and the runs of salmon and other anadromous fish in Pacific Northwest (and Canadian Southwest to Alaska) were being depleted by dam construction, waterway diversions, and destruction of their wetlands spawning habitat. Marine mammals were hunted for lamp oil by non-Natives, who discarded a whale that would feed an entire Native village for the winter in Alaska or Neah Bay or Penobscot Bay, just as buffalo were shot for sport, stripped of their skin, and left to rot, rather than feeding and clothing Native people who were driven to the edge of extinction along with their main food source.

Native Peoples' high-protein, low-fat diets were based on salmon, walleye, trout, catfish, turtle, lobster, shellfish, abalone, deer, antelope, buffalo, elk, moose, squirrel, rabbit, turkey, wild boar, acorns, avocado, cactus, guava, papaya, pawpaw, seaweed, wild rice, taro, camas, yucca, corn, potato, sweet potato, tomatoes, squash, pumpkin, and scores of other gourds, melons, beans, fruit, and berries (including strawberries, blueberries, huckleberries), to name just a few of the foods irrigated, cultivated, grown, hunted, fished, gathered, or eaten raw, smoked, steamed, boiled, broiled, dried, and in stews, soups, salads, breads, and pies.

These rules were imposed without an underlying law, which is highly unusual in American law. For most of the 1800s, Congress appropriated money for the Civilization Fund and the federal Indian Affairs Office awarded Christian denominations exclusive franchises to proselytize to specific Indian tribes under the guise of education and, in 1819, authorized Indian boarding schools. The Civilization rules went much further, making criminal offenses of most distinguishing features that made and make Native Peoples culturally distinct from one another and from non-Natives. Offenders were guilty as charged by the federal Indian agents, without benefit of trial for the accused, who were labeled *troublemaker, ringleader, fomenter of dissent, deviant,* and *hostile.* Among criminal offenses were these:

- **Dancing and giveaways.** Targeted and banned were the Sun Dance "and all other similar dances and so-called religious ceremonies," and the excuse that one is a "mourner" is not a "sufficient or satisfactory answer to any of the offenses." In a later implementing order, issued as an Indian Affairs commissioner circular, federal Indian agents were directed to "undertake a careful propaganda against the Dance." As these rules were vigorously enforced, ceremonial objects, funerary items, and clothing were seized and destroyed, claimed by officers, or distributed to soldiers, and more and more traditional practitioners were jailed and even killed. The dances and ceremonies were driven underground and many never reemerged.

- **Traditional doctors and healing ways.** The Civilization Regulations banned the "usual practices" of a "so-called 'medicine man' [who] operates as a hindrance to the civilization of a tribe," who "resorts to any artifice or device to keep the Indians under his influence," or who "shall use any of the arts of a conjurer to prevent the Indians from abandoning their heathenish rites and customs." In many cases when religious leaders were punished to the breaking point or beyond, many who had sufficient knowledge or agency to continue the practices did so and met the same fate as their predecessors. Yet, others evaded detection and became known as nameless legends imbued with big medicine. Other leaders decided against conducting the ceremonies for fear of endangering their families and practitioners. An untold number of ceremonies ended or were dormant for decades, often long past the mid-1930s withdrawal of the Civilization rules. In this way, the rules succeeded in impeding or halting the exercise of Native religious and spiritual beliefs and instructions, even after they were officially rescinded.

Some sacred ways did not resume until after approval of the American Indian Religious Freedom Act (AIRFA) of 1978, which many practitioners believed made it safe to carry out their ceremonial duties again. The act declared that it "shall be the policy of the United States to protect and preserve for American Indians their inherent right of freedom to believe, express, and exercise the traditional religions of the American Indian, Eskimo, Aleut, and Native Hawaiians, including but not limited to access to sites, use and possession of sacred objects, and the freedom to worship through ceremonials and traditional rites." The AIRFA set the policy stage for follow-on laws regarding protection of Native burial grounds and repatriation of Native remains, funerary items, sacred objects, and cultural patrimony; revitalization of Native American heritage languages; and federal consultation with NativePeoples under the Archaeological Resources Protection Act and the National Historical Preservation Act. In 1994, the AIRFA was amended to provide that the "use, possession, or transportation of peyote by an Indian who uses peyote in a traditional manner for bona fide ceremonial purposes in connection with the practice of a traditional Indian religion is lawful, and shall not be prohibited by the United States or by any State. No Indian shall be penalized or discriminated against on the basis of such use, possession or transportation."

- **Interfering with the "progressive education" of children.** It was a crime for parents or anyone to "adopt any means to prevent the attendance of children at the agency schools," and anyone who tried could be locked up without food. The "progressive education" involved children being removed from their families and homelands to distant places with English-only/Christian-only curricula, military uniforms and regimens, and corporal punishment. The first class of hostage–students was taken in 1879 to the US Army boarding school in Carlisle, Pennsylvania, which was the model for numerous other boarding schools nationwide. This federal system was in place for a century and was a major cause of the emergency status of Native heritage languages today and the historical trauma passed down to the present generations. The goal of the boarding schools was to deculturalize and detribalize the children and to end or lessen their attachment to land, ceremonies, and families, as well as to keep the strong families pacified at home.

- **Roaming away from or "jumping" the reservation.** Leaving the reservation was among the crimes in the Civilization Regulations the US Army took most seriously and the one most likely to spark conflict when the military was called to enforce it. Not only was confinement to the four corners of a reservation a monumental affront to free Native Peoples, but it meant that Native religious practitioners could not travel to conduct place-based ceremonies at off-reservation sites or hold other ceremonies in locations with needed privacy and security. If they did "roam," or "jump," they risked being jailed and starved, sometimes to death, at the discretion of the federal Indian agent. During the Indian Wars, at least one troop of one hundred cavalrymen would be dispatched to round up Indians. Neither the troopers nor the line officers knew the precise motivation or destination of the "hostiles." They only knew that some missing Indians were committing crimes—maybe dancing or escaping—and their mission was to track them into "Indian Country" (which continues to be the Army warfare term for enemy territory), break up any dances, make arrests, collect clothes and paraphernalia associated with "the Dance," and return the prisoners to the reservation for punishment.

"CIVILIZATION" FROM CIBECUE TO WAR TO FORT SILL PRISON

Military and paramilitary civilian entities pursued "civilization" and prosecuted offenses against it before the secretary of the interior issued the 1883 Civilization Regulations. These regulations formalized the reach of "civilization" from Indian and public lands to the entirety of Indian populations throughout and adjacent to the United States. One example of this early "civilization" took place in the late summer of 1881 in eastern Arizona. Arizona was established as a US territory in 1863 after being "acquired" under the 1848 US–Mexico Treaty of Guadalupe Hidalgo and the 1853 Gadsden Purchase (also known as the Treaty of Mesilla) for lands to route a southern railroad line. It was granted statehood in 1912. A US cavalry troop that included twenty-five scouts from two Cibecue Apache Bands was ordered to Cibecue Village to arrest a medicine man and return him to the Fort Apache Reservation of the White Mountain Apache Tribe (Dzil tigai Si'an Ndee, People of the White Mountains) and the Cibecue Apache (Spanish version of Dishchii' Bikoh, Horizontally Red Canyon). White Mountain, Cibecue, and other Apache bands are Western Apache (Ndee and Indé, The People). The US Army moved other Cibecue bands and other tribes to the San Carlos Apache Reservation (San Carlos Tribe, Tsék'áádn, Metate Stone People), with the intent that they would fight one another, rather than the Americans.

The medicine man, Chief Nock-ay-dot-klin-ne (Spotted Mexican, Nakajdotl'ini) of the Cañon Creek Band of the Cibecue Apache, first conducted his ceremonies at Fort Apache, then moved them farther along Cibecue Creek. A visionary known as The Prophet, his ceremonies were attracting increasing numbers of practitioners, which some in the Army chain of command viewed as a budding uprising, even though they permitted their trusted White Mountain Cibecue scouts to participate in the dance. The scouts were directed to ride with their troop, without being told of the mission. When the troop arrested The Prophet at his Cibecue Creek home, the unarmed spiritual leader did not resist, and his adherents were allowed to ride with him to Fort Apache. On the way, the troop was ambushed, The Prophet was wounded, and scouts ignored orders to fire and turned their rifles on their fellow troopers. The troopers retreated with prisoners, including the wounded medicine man, buried him alongside his wife and young son with the troopers who died, and later hanged the scouts as mutineers at the fort.

The Battle of Cibecue sparked the uprising the Army feared. The Chiricahua, Warm Springs, and other Apache bands in Arizona, New Mexico, and northern Mexico joined the White Mountain Apache, including many prominent Apache leaders such as the military and spiritual leader Geronimo (Goyahkla, One Who Yawns), who was Mescalero and Chiricahua of the Bedonkohe Band. The Apache–US war lasted more than two years, during which time most of Goyahkla's Chiricahua Band and family were imprisoned at Fort Marion in St. Augustine, Florida. After Goyahkla's final surrender, he was imprisoned in Texas and elsewhere and not reunited with his Chiricahua people until 1894 in Indian Territory (now, Fort Sill/Lawton in southwest Oklahoma). While prisoners of war, they were treated as harshly as any of their Native contemporaries, and their children were sent to federal Indian boarding schools for year-round "civilization" education. Petitions by the Fort Sill Apache Tribe to return home or to regain their ancestral lands were not granted, and the first of the tribe's elected leaders were born as POWs.

One century after the end of their POW status and following lawsuits affirming their ancestral lands in New Mexico and additional lands in Oklahoma, the Fort Sill Apache Tribe secured some lands, with sacred places, and recognition of their rights in both states. At the same time, almost a century after Goyahkla's passing in 1909, he appeared back in the world news in a most surprising manner. During his lifetime, he was perhaps the most famous of the Indian war leaders, and he became even more widely known when he was paraded as a pacified warrior, always with armed military escorts, at expositions, fairs, inaugural parades, wild west shows, and Indian boarding schools. He has been the subject of books, motion pictures, television programs, and songs, and is so embedded in US military war lore and culture that all paratroopers once were required to shout "Geronimo," when they jumped out of airplanes.

At the White House in 2011, President Barack Obama, Vice President Joseph R. Biden, Secretary of State Hillary Clinton, and US defense and security officials crowded into a small conference area near the Situation Room. They anxiously awaited word from SEAL Team Six in Islamabad, Pakistan, regarding whether Osama bin Laden had been captured or killed. It was the latter: "Geronimo EKIA (enemy killed in action)!" That was the way the world soon would hear the news, including Native veterans, Gold Star families, and children. The code name for bin Laden, the terrorist and US public enemy number one, was "Geronimo." "Enemy killed in action." It was 102 years after Goyahkla left Mother Earth and the news was "Geronimo, Enemy, KIA."

SHERIDAN'S "CIVILIZATION" ON THE SOUTHERN PLAINS, GREAT PLAINS, AND PLATEAU

The last military installation still in operation from the Indian Wars, Fort Sill today is home to Army, Marine Corps, and Air Defense Field Artillery schools and is one of four Army Basic Combat Training sites (including training in operating drones). Fort Sill was sited in 1868 by Major General Philip H. Sheridan for its natural protection on a plateau overlooking prairie land, along Medicine Creek, a tributary of the Red River, in the shadow of a sacred place, Medicine Bluff, on the edge of the Wichita Mountains.

Sheridan was an acolyte of the "total war" strategy, even before Union Army Major General William Tecumseh Sherman's late-1864 March to the Sea through Georgia from the burning of Atlanta to the capture and sacking of Savannah. Earlier, Commanding General of the US Army Ulysses S. Grant ordered Sheridan to turn Virginia's Shenandoah Valley into "barren waste." Sheridan began burning four hundred square miles of what was called the Confederacy's breadbasket—crops, food stores, fields, barns, and mills were burned; animals were slaughtered; and wells, waterworks, factories, and railroads were destroyed. A Civil War hero, Sheridan relentlessly pursued Robert E. Lee, commander-in-chief of the Confederate forces, to his defeat at Appomattox and 1865 surrender to Grant.

After Grant was promoted to the new, congressionally established rank of General of the Army of the United States, he chose Sheridan in 1867 to pacify and control hostile Indians and to protect settlers on the southern Plains. Among the Native Peoples who were removed to the Red River area in the early 1800s were the Caddo Nation and Wichita Tribes. The Caddo (Hasinai; "Caddo" is a French version of the word Kadohadacho, True Chiefs) and numerous bands were part of three confederacies—Hasinai, Kadohadacho, and Natchitoches— who were forced out of their homelands by the Louisiana Purchase. Caddo Mounds have been raided and razed in their ancestral lands, not only in Louisiana, but in Arkansas and Texas as well. The third Caddo removal was from Texas to Oklahoma, accompanied by Anadarko and Hasinai Peoples, who were located at the Wichita Reservation upon arrival. Once the Civil War broke out, the Anadarkos fled to Kansas but were misidentified as Caddos and returned to Oklahoma.

The Wichita and Affiliated Tribes are Wichita (Guichitas, Kitikiti'sh, "raccoon-eyed people," for their face tattoos, or Kitikiti's, People of the Cross Timbers); Waco (Hueco or Huaco; Keechi (K'itaish, Kitsai, Kichai); Tawakoni (Quiscat and Flechazos Villages); and descendants of other relatives, Taovayan, Tawehash, and Tehuacana. They are Indigenous Peoples of and removed from what are now Kansas, Texas, and Oklahoma. The Wichita Peoples' Medicine Stone, a large meteorite near the Taovayan villages, was stolen in 1806 by white men, including a trader and a federal Indian agent. Smallpox and other epidemics reduced their numbers and weakened the living, beginning the Days of Darkness that lasted more than a century and included Confederate soldiers driving them into Kansas, where they lived in great hardship from 1863 to 1867.

This is only a miniscule glimpse of the state of Native Peoples of the area when Sheridan arrived with his scorched earth fervor. His command at Fort Sill included the Seventh US Cavalry (the "Garryowen") under Lieutenant Colonel George A. Custer (Sheridan's trusted Civil War friend); the Tenth US Cavalry (eventually the four Black Buffalo Soldier regiments served there and built Camp Wichita), under Colonel Benjamin Grierson; and the Nineteenth Kansas Volunteers and Sixth US Infantry. Among the Native Peoples in the Red River region at that time were the Arapaho (Hinono'ei, Blue Sky People, Blue Clouds), Cheyenne (Tsistsistas, Tsetsehestahese, Human Beings, The People), Comanche (Numunuu, The People; "Comanche" is a Spanish version of the Ute word Komántcia, Enemy or Anyone Who Wants to Fight Me All the Time), and Kiowa (Kai-i-gwu, Principal People).

Custer carried out Sheridan's total war strategy in the winter 1868–69 campaign against the Cheyenne, Arapaho, Kiowa, and Comanche Nations, plus other nations camped along the Washita River, all of whom had signed treaties with the United States in 1867 at Medicine Lodge Creek. The scorched earth campaign started with the November 1868 assault against the Cheyenne in the Washita (Lodgepole, Tall Pines) Valley. Custer attacked the camp of Peace Chief Black Kettle (Moke-tav-a-to; Cheyenne: Suhtai, So'taeo'o, So'taetaneo'o), who was a signer of the 1867 Cheyenne–Arapaho–US Medicine Lodge Creek Treaty. In the November 1864 Sand Creek Massacre by the Colorado Volunteer Cavalry. Cheyenne and Arapaho elderly chiefs, young mothers, pregnant women, and children were murdered or mutilated. Custer's men killed and maimed people, killed hundreds of ponies, and burned all the lodges, medicines, and winter blankets, clothes, foods, seeds, and supplies. Screams of people and animals went on all night. Chief Black Kettle and his wife, *Ar-no-ho-wok* (Medicine Woman hereafter), escaped, only to be killed at the Washita four years later.

Sheridan's command chased "hostiles" all over the Plains, in formulaic attacks on camps of sleeping families, pursuit of some people who were escaping on horseback, leaving everything behind. The soldiers took what they wanted, then set fire to all lodges and piles of apparel, hunting and cooking utensils, paints and medicines, and pipes and pipe bags. Army archival records of raids are replete with exact numbers of captured moccasins, buckskin shirts and dresses, buffalo robes, beaded strips, winter and summer counts, toys, dolls, weapons, water pails, cooking pots, cradleboards, travois, containers of dried meat and corn, live and dead horses and dogs and other animals, and bodies and body parts of men, women, and children.

Records also were kept of exact, reported, or estimated numbers of buffalo killed by white bounty hunters, soldiers, and civilians. Buffalo-kill tourism was a popular sport on trains moving across the Plains, with white men and women shooting rifles out the train windows as they rolled past a buffalo herd. US Army records put the slaughter of buffalo at thirty-one million between 1868 and 1881. Sheridan was especially proud of the killed buffalo (which he called the Indians' "commissary" and the key to killing off the Indians). In testimony before a legislative committee in Texas in 1875, Sheridan stated, "Send them powder and lead, if you will; but, for the sake of a lasting peace, let them kill, skin, and sell until the buffaloes are exterminated. Then your prairies can be covered with speckled cattle, and the festive cowboy, who follows the hunter as a second forerunner of an advanced civilization. ('You kill the buffalo, you destroy the Indian's commissary.')"

Sherman wrote in an 1868 letter, "But the more [Indians] we can kill this year, the less will have to be killed the next war. For the more I see of these Indians the more convinced am I that they have all to be killed, or be maintained as a species of paupers."

After the Cheyenne camp along the Washita was burned to the ground, Custer's men moved the captives, fifty-three women and children, to Camp Supply. The Washita prisoners would be moved twice more, to Fort Cobb then to Fort Sill. Kiowas called Fort Sill Tso-Kada-Hagya, Where the Soldiers Live at Medicine Bluff. First called Camp Medicine Bluff or Camp Wichita, Sheridan renamed the installation Fort Sill in 1869, after his West Point and Civil War friend, General Joshua W. Sill, who was killed in 1862 at Stone River, Tennessee. Medicine Bluff is held sacred by most of the Native Peoples in the region, including the Comanche, Arapaho, Caddo, Cheyenne, and Kiowa Nations.

A plaque at Medicine Bluff lets visitors know that the cliff is 310 feet high and that the sick were brought there to be healed. The Medicine Creek bluffs were also where "young braves fasted in lonely vigils seeking visions of the supernatural, and warriors presented their shields to the rising sun for power." According to the plaque, the bluff was also a legendary place for Native suicides.

When Grant was president and Sherman became commander-in-chief of the US Army, Sheridan became responsible for protecting settlers and for enforcing peace with Indians throughout the vast territory under the US Department of the Missouri. Among the Native Peoples he impacted were the following:

- Assiniboine and Gros Ventre Tribes of the Fort Belknap Indian Tribes
- Fort Belknap Indian Community of the *Nakoda* and *Aaniiih* Nations (*Atsina, A'aninin,* White Clay People; *Nakoda,* Generous Ones)
- Blackfeet Tribe of the Blackfeet Indian Reservation of Montana (*Niitsitapi,* the Original People; *Siksikaitsitapi,* Blackfoot-Speaking Real People; *Amskapi Pikani, Piegan* Blackfeet of the Blackfoot Confederacy)
- Crow Tribe of Indians (*Apsaalooke,* Children of the Large-Beaked Bird)
- Great Sioux Nation (*Oceti Sakowin; the* Sioux *Lakota, Dakota, and Nakota Peoples*). "Sioux" is a French version of an Anishinaabe word, *Nadowessioux,* "little snakes."
- Iowa Tribe of Kansas and Nebraska; Iowa Tribe of Oklahoma (*Bah-Kho-Je* or *Baxoje,* Grey Snow)
- Kaw Nation (*Kansa,* name of a Siouan dialect)

- Mandan, Hidatsa, and Arikara Nation (previously, Three Affiliated Tribes of the Fort Berthold Indian Reservation); Mandan (*Miiti Naamni*), Hidatsa (*Awadi Aguraawi*), Arikara (Acitaanu')
- Omaha Tribe of Nebraska (Umo'ho', Upstream People, "against the current")
- Osage Nation (Wah-Zah-Zhe, Water People). Osage is a French version of *Wah-Zah-Zhe*. Previously, the Osage were Ni-u-kon-ska, Children of the Middle Waters.
- Otoe-Missouria Tribe of Indians. "Missouria" is from an Algonquian term, 8emessourit, People with Canoes Made of Logs, dugout canoes.
- Pawnee Nation and Chaui "Grand," Kitkehahki "Republican," Pitahawirata "Tappage," and Skidi "Wolf" Bands (Chaticks-Si-Chaticks, Men of Men. "Pawnee," from the Lakota word for "horn" (*pariki* or *parrico*) referred to the way Pawnee men wore their hair like a curved horn.
- Ponca Tribe of Indians of Oklahoma and Ponca Tribe of Nebraska (Ponca, Those Who Lead; Clan name of Kansa, Osage, and Quapaw)
- Quapaw Nation (O-Gah-Pah, Downstream People)
- Winnebago Tribe of Nebraska (Hochungra, People of the Parent Speak)

More than a century after the carnage, the US Congress established the Washita Battlefield National Historic Site in 1996 and the Sand Creek Massacre National Historic Site in 2000, and passed the Little Bighorn Battlefield National Monument Act of 1991, which dropped Custer's name from the site. In 2023 in Colorado, the US Board on Geographic Names changed the name of Mount Evans (named after the former Colorado governor largely responsible for the attack against the Peace Camp along the Sand Creek) to Mount Blue Sky (for the Cheyenne Blue Sky renewal ceremony and the Arapaho Blue Sky People).

As a three-star lieutenant general in charge of all the land from the Mississippi River to the Rocky Mountains, Sheridan is credited with keeping scores of Great Plains, Great Basin, and Plateau Native Nations from their spiritual, medicinal, subsistence, and treaty places in the mountain peaks, waterfalls, volcano caldera, lava flows, grasslands, lakes, rivers, geysers, hot springs, and boiling mud landscapes and viewscapes (plus obsidian and commercial areas, including obsidian used by the distant Cody and Hopewell Peoples) of Yellowstone National Park.

Covering two million acres of Wyoming, Montana, and Idaho, Yellowstone is known to various Native Peoples in descriptors that translate to English as the "land of the burning ground" or "land of vapors" (Crow, Apsalooke), as "many smoke" (Blackfeet), as "smoke from the ground" (Salish and Kootenai), and as "the place of hot water" (Kiowa). In the Hidatsa language, it is called Mi tsi a-da-zi (Yellow Stone River). Gold was struck on Yellowstone's northwestern edge in 1862, it became the first national park in 1872, and the US Army Cavalry patrolled the park from 1886 to 1918 to safeguard the park and tourists, and to prevent Native Peoples, railroads, miners, vandals, and other trespassers and developers from entering the park.

In this decade, the National Park Service has identified fewer than thirty "associated tribes" to consult with regarding matters affecting Yellowstone. However, the number of Native Peoples confirmed to have connections to Yellowstone through oral history and the existing literature far exceeds thirty, and ongoing studies in academia and various federal entities suggest that even more should be in the consulting class of "associated tribes."

Native Peoples retained and retain rights in these off-reservation sacred and subsistence landscapes. They were and are usual and customary places for ceremonies, fishing, gathering, or hunting on lands explicitly and implicitly reserved in ceded territories. Notwithstanding the facts of Native Peoples' original, ancestral, and use rights, Native lands and even parts of their reservations were confiscated and declared to be in the public domain, public lands, or federal property. The Natives' so-called abandonment of and disinterest in these lands was used to justify the taking of them, with no acknowledgment that "roaming away from the reservations" was forbidden by the same federal entities now asserting jurisdiction and ownership of the "abandoned" lands. Over time, these lands were designated variously as areas for the following activities, to name but a few: agriculture and animal experimentation, antiquities monuments, archives digitization and storage, archaeological and historical sites preservation, atomic and nuclear energy and weapons research and testing, battlefield memorials, battle equipment and uniform manufacturing plants, botanical gardens, bridges and tunnels, coastal and submerged sites, cemeteries, combat staging and training camps, conservation zones and pathways, dams, defense and language schools, ecosystem restoration zones, geothermal energy and hydropower facilities, green energy and minerals development quarries, environmental cleanup projects, evacuation facilities and routes, fairs and expositions, fish and wildlife preserves, forests and logging roads, government buildings and housing, habitats, highways and transportation systems, hospitals and treatment centers, military equipment and uniform manufacturing plants, military posts, mines and mining activities, national security, oil and gas reserves, parks, pastureland, radioactive waste repositories, recreation, refuges, sanctuaries, scientific research and resources, space exploration, superfund sites, surplus land and property, telescopes (giant, space-based), tidal and nontidal wetlands, tidelands and coastal waters, tourism, universities, war mobilization and production, water projects, weather and atmospheric stations, wildernesses, wind farms, and zoos.

DESECRATING NATIVE SACRED PLACES BY SUBSTITUTING SLURS

In addition to simply renaming Native Peoples, the various colonizers knew the effect of desecration over degradation and systematically changed names of Native sacred places and historic sites to pejoratives, saints' names, or words associated with the Christian devil and hell. These acts of renaming were the most demoralizing and injurious ways that Euro-Americans expressed racial superiority, reinforced the "right of discovery," and conveyed new ownership of land and "naming rights." Even later reformers justified these slurs on the sacred, claiming that they helped keep Native Peoples afraid of and away from their most important areas and made it easier to Christianize individuals and retain and manage stolen lands.

One of the pejoratives commonly used to demean important cultural landscapes and land and water features was *sq**w*, a term or root word in certain Iroquoian and Algonquian languages to refer to women's private body parts. It was first used to demean Native women who lived with or married English and French trappers, then all Native women, then women generally. As it was popularized and moved from denigrating persons to desecrating place-names, it began to show up as names of mascots and cheerleaders, then of women in "men's sports." That is when some Native leaders made early strides toward stopping its use generally. Clan mothers and chiefs of the Seneca and Mohawk Nations, on behalf of all Haudenosaunee, began a concerted effort in the 1970s to convince leaders of cities, towns, and universities in New York to stop using the word as a location descriptor or a team name. Their first success was with the Brown Sq**w women's sports team at St. Bonaventure University, where the men's team was the Brown Indians. The women players and their coaches stopped using the word immediately after its meaning was explained, while it would take almost twenty more years for the men to drop the Brown Indian team name. By the mid-1980s, the S-word had been eliminated from American sports.

The anti-sq**w cause was picked up by Native Peoples throughout the United States, who made the point about the word's meaning, as well as the fact that the word has never been an honorific of any kind and is both racist and sexist. As the decolonization effort gained greater attention, a counteroffensive was launched by a white male linguist at the Smithsonian Institution and the Wampanoag woman he "taught" to reconstruct and speak her Wôpanâak language long after it was no longer spoken by her Wampanoag People. They claimed it was a respectable term that merely meant "woman."

Despite disinformation and opposition, the S-word has been dropped from geographic locations, most notably in favor of Piestewa Peak in Phoenix, Arizona, named to honor the first American woman to die in combat in the Iraq War, Army Specialist Lori Piestewa (Hopi; 1979–2003). At the urging of Native activists, Governor Janet Napolitano and the Arizona State Board on Geographic and Historic Names changed the desert mountain's name in 2003 and, after the mandatory five-year wait, the US Board on Geographic Names made the new name official in 2008. Other prominent renamings include Unity Island in Buffalo, New York (2015); Skenoh (a Seneca word for peace or health) Island in Canandaigua Lake, Canandaigua, New York (2021); Palisades Tahoe (Edge of Lake in the language of the Washoe Tribe, whose women led the effort), Olympic Valley, California (2021); and Yokuts (People) Valley in Fresno County, California (2023).

Former Maine Governor Angus King approved a bill mandating the renaming of all natural landmarks, mountains, waters, and townships containing the offensive word (2021). Similar statewide actions have also been taken in California, Idaho, Minnesota, Montana, Oregon, and South Dakota. At the end of 2021, US Secretary of the Interior Deb Haaland (Laguna Pueblo) issued an order for the US Board on Geographic Names to review and rename locations on federal lands with derogatory names, such as the S-word, and more than 650 were changed in 2022. Precedents for the order include Interior Secretary Stewart Udall's identification of the N-word as derogatory and order for the elimination of its use (1962), and the Board on Geographic Names' decision to replace a pejorative term for Japanese people (1974).

The best-known focus of the devil-and-hell renamings is a mountain in northeastern Wyoming called Devils Tower, which was designated the first US national monument in 1906. Its image is known worldwide, primarily from the ultimate tourist destination film, Steven Spielberg's *Close Encounters of the Third Kind* (1977). Long before movies, Wyoming, or the United States existed, Devils Tower was a holy place. For many Native Peoples, it continues to be a ceremonial area, origin site, and place of visions and remembrance. Those who hold it sacred have names for it in their own languages, among them the Arapaho (Woox-niii-non, Bear's Tipi); Cheyenne (Na Kovea, Bear Lodge); Crow (Dax-pitcheeaasaao, Home of Bears); Kiowa (T'sou'a'e, Aloft on a Rock); Lakota (Mato Tipil'a, Bear's Tipi); and Mandan (Tso-I-E, Rock Tree). These nations and others are trying to change the name to Bear Lodge, Bear Medicine Lodge, or Bear's Tipi.

Another example involves sacred Wallowa (fish net tripod) lands of the Nez Perce and Umatilla Peoples in the Wallowa Valley of Idaho, home of Chief Joseph's Band. Of particular concern are Hells Canyon and the Seven Devils Mountains, whose separate peaks are called such names as He Devil, She Devil, Devils Throne, Tower of Babel, The Ogre, Mount Baal, Black Imp, and The Goblin.

An active volcano and the highest mountain of the Cascade Range, Mount Rainier is sacred to many Native Peoples of the Pacific Northwest, but was renamed for a British admiral who fought against the Americans in the Revolutionary War. Royal Navy Captain George Vancouver, who named the mountain Rainier, charted much of the Northwest coast of British Columbia, Alaska, Washington, Oregon, and California, as well as Hawai'i and Australia. As mentioned earlier in this article, a movement is underway to revert to the mountain's Puyallup name, Tahoma, Mother of Waters.

An Apache sacred place, Dzil Nchaa Si'an, Big Seated Mountain, is known to non-Natives as Mount Graham and has been desecrated by the Vatican Telescope project, precluding Apache emergence ceremonies and disturbing the Ga'an, Mountain Spirits, Crown Dancers, who live there—renamed Devil Dancers by non-Natives in Arizona. The US Forest Service, the University of Arizona, and other developers went to great lengths to fast-track the telescope project, including publicizing a statement by an Arizona priest representing the Vatican claiming that the mountain was not a sacred place. The university made secret payments to the then-chairman of the San Carlos Apache Tribe, who denounced Apache Survival organization leaders and tribal citizens, falsely claiming they were lying. He testified to Congress that the mountain was not sacred to the Apache People, which gave federal and state developers time to lobby the Arizona congressional delegation to secure a 1988 appropriations rider directing that the telescope project would be built, "notwithstanding any other provision of law." The duplicity only came to light during a later federal trial of the chairman for embezzling tribal funds. In 2005, tribal and traditional leaders of all the Apache tribes issued a joint Declaration of Apache Cultural Property, part of which stated that Mount Graham was and is an Apache sacred place. The mountain's current name honors Colonel James Duncan Graham, who fought in the Second Seminole War, was a founder of the Army Corps of Topographical Engineers, directed the re-survey of the Mason-Dixon line, and was principal astronomer and led the demarcation of the U.S–Mexico boundary under the Treaty of Guadalupe Hidalgo.

San Francisco Peaks is among the many Native sacred places named after Catholic saints. The peaks are held sacred by Hopi, Navajo, Acoma, Apache, Havasupai, Hualapai, Mojave, Southern Paiute, Yavapai, and Zuni Peoples, who all have names for the peaks in their languages, but Franciscans renamed the peaks to honor their founder, Saint Francis of Assisi. The US Forest Service and other developers permit use of wastewater to make snow for private ski businesses and other activities that defile the spiritual well-being of and pose health dangers for the Native adherents. Numerous Native lawsuits have been filed during the past half century, but the United States has sided with the private enterprises, and the judicial decisions have been used to guide Forest Service policies and decisions affecting Native Peoples.

The Forest Service and the Bureau of Land Management have permitted private companies to conduct preliminary drilling explorations for what would be an enormous open copper pit in the Santa Rita Mountains, over the objections of the Tohono O'odham Nation and the Hopi and Pascua Yaqui Tribes. The origin of the mountain range's name has to do with a white marble streak on one cliff that reminded missionaries of an Italian nun with a scarred forehead, Saint Rita of Cascia; of course, the mountains have had an O'odham name since time immemorial, Ce:wi Do'ag, Long Mountain, and its name translates to "beautiful" in other Native languages. The range's twenty-seven peaks contain myriad ceremonial, burial, observance, and historical areas that could be desecrated or severely damaged by the copper mining, which remains in litigation. Also in litigation, with the Supreme Court's denial of a review off the appellate ruling against the Apache Stronghold, is another proposed Arizona copper mine whose crater would dwarf all others and would raze much of the sacred place known as Oak Flat, Chi'chil Bildagoteel (Place Where the Emory Oak Grows), although the place renamed Devil's Canyon would remain untouched.

YOSEMITE: FROM MIWOK LAND TO NATIONAL PARK

Sometimes a place-name would be obviously related to the feature's appearance in the landscape, such as Yosemite National Park's massive granite cliff and rock formation, El Capitan ("the captain" in Spanish), whose original name in the language of the Southern Sierra Miwok (*miwwik*, People; also Me-Wuk, Miwuk, and Mi-Wuk) is To-tock-ahn-oo-lah (Rock Chief; Tutokanula). Located in central California in the western Sierra Nevada, Yosemite encompasses 1,200 square miles, 94 percent of which is a designated wilderness area. It features ancient giant sequoia groves, old-growth forests, two designated Wild and Scenic Rivers, wetlands, and a dozen waterfalls, including one of the tallest in North America and the world, Yosemite Falls, and the one that falls off Rock Chief/El Capitan and looks like a thousand-foot-long ribbon of fire as it reflects midwinter sunsets (a natural phenomenon at Horsetail Falls for only two weeks annually, in late February).

Home to the Tuolumne (Miwok, Talmalamne, Many Stone Homes) River, Meadows, Canyon, and watershed (the source of San Francisco's drinking water), Yosemite's glaciated valley (Ahwahne, Gaping Mouth Place) is the ancestral home of the Miwok Band (Ahwahneechee, People of the Ahwahne). On the valley floor, the Ahwahneechee fished for trout and salmon, gathered acorns and manzanita berries, hunted deer, and cultivated foods and medicines. In the bottomlands, they harvested fiber plants, bark, and grapevines for baskets, hats, shoes, clothing, and houses. Higher in the foothills, they hunted birds, mountain sheep, and other animals. They conducted place-based ceremonies throughout the valley and surrounding areas, living this way from time immemorial until Euro-American "civilization" entered their territory in the early 1800s. "By 1910," according to the National Park Service website, "over 90% of the original *Ahwahneechee* inhabitants were dead or missing."

Here is how it happened to the Ahwahneechee and their Miwok, Mono, and Northern Paiute relatives and other Native Peoples. Once the Louisiana Purchase was concluded in 1803, President Thomas Jefferson commissioned his secretary, Meriwether Lewis, a naturalist, to organize the Corps of Discovery to explore and map the Louisiana Territory along the Missouri River, from St. Louis into the American West and beyond (through Oregon to the Pacific Ocean). Lewis added to the expedition a friend he had served with in the US Army, William Clark, a mapmaker and recordkeeper. Lewis enlisted more cartographers, surveyors, and other colleagues from the University of Pennsylvania, as well as frontiersmen such as Toussaint Charbonneau and his pregnant wife, a Shoshone interpreter, Sacagawea (Boat Puller, or Sakakawea, Bird Woman). The only woman on the expedition, she worked the same way as the men, but she did so while pregnant and carrying her newborn son and toddler. The corps—whose members numbered thirty-three plus the child, Jean Baptiste Charbonneau—mapped, named, and recorded myriad new mountains, land features, waterways, animals, birds, water life, trees, and plants (that is, new to them, but not to *Sacagawea* or to the many distinct Native Peoples they met).

Non-Native incursions spawned by the Corps began in 1810 in the San Joaquin Valley, not far from Yosemite, causing an upheaval in the lives and ways of Miwok, Mono, Paiute, Pomo, Shoshone, Washoe, Wintun, and Yokut Peoples. Settlers and foreign diseases ravaged the Native populations and forced many frantic families and small groups of individuals to higher ground and into Yosemite and other nearby valleys and foothills. This tumultuous push toward Indian extinction increased steadily until 1849, when news of the California gold rush spread like wildfire, and speculators and settlers blazed trails to strike sites, burning anyone and anything in their way. California's first elected governor, a white former Tennessee slave owner, Peter Hardeman Burnett, declared in his 1851 State of the State Address, "That a war of extermination will continue to be waged between the two races until the Indian race becomes extinct must be expected." California officials and mining companies took actions to either move or mow down Native persons, including paying bounties for dead Indians. Native groups organized across tribal lines and fought back, and miners in and around Mariposa ("butterfly" in Spanish) formed the Mariposa Battalion, a state-sponsored militia that killed Indians and burned their houses and multiyear food stores, to drive the living out of Yosemite Valley. Mariposa was a gold-strike town and area close to Arch Rock on the northeast edge of the valley, places at the center of the California gold rush and the Mariposa Indian War of 1850–51.

The valley was named Yosemite by Lafayette H. Bunnell of the Mariposa Battalion, who stuck it rich from placer gold and mills. Bunnell thought he was naming the valley after the Ahwahneechee Band of Miwok, not knowing they had called the various invaders of their homelands Yosemite, meaning "they are killers" in Miwok. Bunnell later wrote about the naming (the internal quotation marks are his own):

> As I did not take a fancy to any of the names proposed, I remarked that "an American name would be the most appropriate"; that "I could not see any necessity for going to a foreign country for a name for American scenery—the grandest that had ever yet been looked upon. . . . That it would be better to give it an Indian name than to import a strange and inexpressive one; that the name of the tribe who had occupied it, would be more appropriate than any I had heard suggested." I then proposed "that we give the valley the name of Yo-sem-i-ty, as it was suggestive, euphonious, and certainly American; that by so doing, the name of the tribe of Indians which we met leaving their homes in this valley, perhaps never to return, would be perpetuated." . . . upon a viva voce vote being taken, it was almost unanimously adopted.

To address the carnage of Indians in California, US President Millard Fillmore nominated, the Senate confirmed, and Congress funded three US treaty commissioners to negotiate agreements for Native Peoples to exchange land for reservations and protection against further encroachment. At the same time, California authorized more than $1 million to fund the Indian-hunting militia campaigns. As the US commissioners were meeting with tribal leaders in southern and northern California and treaty-making was underway, the new state legislature petitioned the US Senate not to ratify the treaties. Even before the commissioners finished drawing up the treaties, and despite their increasingly desperate letters urging ratification and reporting on the dire situation of those who signed the treaties, the Senate went into executive session and voted against the eighteen unratified treaties in California.

In 1864, President Abraham Lincoln signed the Yosemite Grant Act to preserve the valley and the Mariposa grove of giant sequoias for "public use, resort, and recreation," and the land was placed under California's jurisdiction as a state park. Yosemite National Park was established in 1890, but California retained partial control, under which the valley was overgrazed by sheep and overrun by tourists, and a railroad was almost allowed to run through it. In 1906, the national park was proclaimed to be unified under federal jurisdiction and the US Army was put in charge, with management transferred to the National Park Service upon its formation in 1916. The park was expanded a few times and most of it is the Yosemite Wilderness, protected in its natural state. In 1984, the United Nations designated Yosemite National Park as a UNESCO World Heritage Site.

NATIVE RELIGIOUS FREEDOM AND CULTURAL RIGHTS IN CALIFORNIA

The United States and California continue to attempt to make amends for their actions, which caused two centuries of devastation to the Native Peoples of the Yosemite and San Joaquin regions and elsewhere in the state. California's Native American Heritage Commission, established in 1976, identifies and catalogs Native American ancestral, cultural, and sacred sites on public lands; ensures access to sacred sites and prevents irreparable damage to them; and guards against interference with the expression of Native American religion in California. The commission's work has helped Native Peoples to validate their eligibility for state and federal recognitions and programs, which help was essential in light of disrupted Native lives and the destruction of most documents needed to demonstrate tribal existence.

G-O ROAD, THE FOREST SERVICE, AND SECRETARY LYNG

In the 1970s in the high country of Northern California, traditional religious leaders and practitioners of the Karuk, Tolowa, and Yurok Tribes were using vision questing and healing sites and other ceremonial areas as they had for many generations. Some of these ceremonies were conducted in the Chimney Rock area of the Six Rivers National Forest. The US Forest Service wanted to build a logging road between the towns of Gasquet and Orleans (the G-O road), which would run through the ceremonial areas. Tribes, environmental organizations, and concerned individuals sued US Agriculture Secretary Richard E. Lyng to stop the road from being built. They won lower court decisions, which found that the road would burden and violate tribal rights under the free exercise of religion clause of the First Amendment and that the logging road did not serve a compelling governmental interest that would justify such a violation. However, the US Supreme Court in 1988 ruled that the building of the road and promotion of logging did not violate tribal free exercise of religion rights under the First Amendment to the US Constitution. However, most justices stated that the road would be "potentially destructive of the very core of Northwest religious beliefs and practices," restating the conclusion of the Forest Service's own expert anthropologist. Indeed, this expert's report recommended that the road not be built and that the area instead be nominated for the National Register of Historic Places. The Forest Service ignored this recommendation.

The plaintiffs pinned their hopes on the first Amendment to the US Constitution and on the American Indian Religious Freedom Act, but the Supreme Court found that neither was a door to the courthouse for Native Peoples seeking to protect our sacred places. That finding meant that everyone else in the United States could use the Constitution to go to court to protect their churches. Only Native Peoples cannot. The decision—unfortunately written by the first woman on the high court—also stated that the Native view of the sacred was simply too expansive. The decision also suggested that Congress should act on this issue. It has been thirty-seven years since that decision and, despite repeated attempts, Congress has not considered a course of action to protect sacred places. Every time we would begin to garner attention on the Hill, there would be the Forest Service, dogging us and telling the staff or member that what we wanted was veto bait.

As it turned out, the G-O road was quietly stopped by having the sites included in a larger area with protected status, so the Native Peoples in California got what they wanted, but the entire decision has been awful for any Native People trying to protect our sacred places.

STRENGTHENING TRIBES
THROUGH GAMING

Often, the state has not been in sync with the goals of strengthening Native tribes, most notably in 1986, when California tried to shut down bingo and card games on lands of two Cahuilla tribes near Palm Springs, the Cabazon and Morongo Bands of Mission Indians, because state law did not allow gambling. The US Supreme Court decided the case in favor of the bands in 1987, in a landmark decision which ruled that the bands' inherent sovereignty was legally sufficient to operate gaming businesses. This decision opened the way for tribal gaming and profits in and outside California. States demanded that Congress overrule the high court's decision, until they were provided a way of being cut into the rapidly increasing income stream in the 1988 Indian Gaming Regulatory Act, which established the National Indian Gaming Commission to exercise oversight of state and tribal conduct.

CALIFORNIA GOVERNOR'S APOLOGY

In 2019, California Governor Gavin Newsom apologized on behalf of California to Native American Peoples in California "for the many instances of violence, mistreatment and neglect inflicted upon [them] throughout the state's history. . . . It's called genocide. That's what it was, a genocide. No other way to describe it." He also announced the creation of a "Truth and Healing Council to provide an avenue for California Native Americans to clarify the record . . . on the troubled relationship between tribes and the state." The governor continued, "California must reckon with our dark history. California Native American peoples suffered violence, discrimination and exploitation sanctioned by state government throughout its history. We can never undo the wrongs inflicted on the peoples who have lived on this land that we now call California since time immemorial, but we can work together to build bridges, tell the truth about our past and begin to heal deep wounds."

Among the descendant Native Peoples to the Yosemite Peoples are: The original territory of the **Bishop Paiute Tribe** (Numu, The People, or Nimi, People includes the Owens Valley, located at the base of the eastern Sierra Nevada. **Bridgeport Indian Colony**, also located in the eastern Sierra, consists of descendants from the Miwok, Mono, Paiute, Shoshone, and Washoe Peoples. **Northfork Rancheria of Mono Indians** (Nim, People) also comprises descendants of Yokut and Miwok Peoples. This tribe was named by non-Natives after Northfork, California, near the Sierra National Forest and the San Joaquin Valley use area. **Picayune Rancheria of Chukchansi Indians** is indigenous to what is now Madera County, California, and lived on the edges of the San Joaquin Valley and the foothills of the Sierra Nevada for millennia. **Tachi Yokut Tribe** (Nim, People) of the Santa Rosa Rancheria, and the Santa Rosa Indian Community of the Santa Rosa Rancheria, were also once joint users of the San Joaquin Valley.

Among the descendant Native Peoples with existing federal-tribal relationships are the **Buena Vista Rancheria of Me-Wuk Indians**; **California Valley Miwok Tribe** (formerly, Sheep Ranch Rancheria of Me-Wuk Indians); **Chicken Ranch Rancheria of Me-Wuk Indians**; **Federated Indians of Graton Rancheria** (formerly, Federated Coast Miwok); **Ione Band of Miwok Indians** (Ione, California); **Jackson Band of Miwuk Indians** (formerly, Jackson Rancheria of Me-Wuk Indians); **Middletown Rancheria of**

Pomo Indians, comprised of Pomo, Lake Miwok, and Wintun descendants; **Shingle Springs Band of Miwok Indians, Shingle Springs Rancheria (Verona Tract); Tuolumne Band of Me-Wuk Indians of the Tuolumne Rancheria; United Auburn Indian Community of the Auburn Rancheria;** and **Wilton Rancheria**. Still others are striving to reestablish federal-tribal relationships.

SÁTTÍTLA HIGHLANDS AND CHUCKWALLA NATIONAL MONUMENTS

On January 7, 2025, President Joseph R. Biden signed two proclamations protecting Native sacred places in California: the Sáttítla Highlands and the Chuckwalla. The Sáttítla Highlands National Monument, northeast of Mount Shasta in Northern California, encompasses more than 224,000 acres and parts of the Modoc, Shasta-Trinity, and Klamath National Forests. The Sáttítla Highlands include the ancestral homelands of the Pit River Tribe and Modoc Peoples. Also known as Medicine Lake and Medicine Lake Highlands, the Sáttítla is held sacred by the Pit River, Modoc, Karuk, Klamath, Shasta, Siletz, Wintu, and Yana Peoples. The White House fact sheet states, "This designation honors the sacred cultural value of these lands, while protecting the area's rich ecological, scientific, and historical significance. . . . Much of the rain that falls on the area filters through the porous volcanic rock recharging underground aquifers that are essential for protecting and storing clean water for Northern California communities."

The Pit River Tribe has been in litigation for decades, attempting to halt proposed geothermal development of Medicine Lake and Medicine Lake Highlands. A Pit River belief is that, after Mother Earth was created, the Creator and his son bathed in Medicine Lake, whose clear blue waters have healing powers. Sáttítla is a spiritual center for the Pit River and Modoc Tribes, who continue to use the area for religious activities, ceremonies, and gatherings.

The Chuckwalla National Monument protects more than 624,000 acres of land in Southern California, preserving critical habitat for imperiled and rare species, and ensuring the ancestral homelands and sacred cultural legacies of the region's Tribal Nations endure for generations to come. The new monument protects the ancestral homelands and cultural landscapes of the Cahuilla, Chemehuevi, Mojave, Quechan, and Serrano Nations, and other Indigenous Peoples.

The White House fact sheet describes the Chuckwalla National Monument in these terms:

> [the] monument boundary includes five distinct areas that
> together encompass sacred sites, ancient trails, historic
> properties, cultural areas, religious sites, petroglyphs,

geoglyphs, and pictographs, honoring and safeguard-
ing the cultural and spiritual value inherent with these
lands. . . . Located just south of Joshua Tree National
Park, the Chuckwalla [is] at the confluence of the Mojave
and Colorado Deserts, showcasing an awe-inspiring
landscape of mountain ranges, meandering canyons and
washes, dramatic rock formations, palm oases, and desert-
wash woodlands. Its natural wonders include the Painted
Canyon of Mecca Hills, where visitors can wind through
towering rock walls and marvel at the landscape's dramatic
geologic history.

SPECIAL ISSUE OF THE
WICAZO SA REVIEW

This special issue of the *Wicazo Sa Review* grew out of the 2021–23
Sacred Places Protection Project conducted by the Native American
Rights Fund and the Morning Star Institute. During a virtual gathering of Native traditional knowledge bearers, scholars, and advocates,
Wicazo Sa Review editor Lloyd L. Lee (Diné) offered to devote journal pages to Native writings on issues involving sacred places. Many
people offered to write and had excellent topics and the best of inten-
tions. Alas, our population still is not large enough to have a great pool
of people who can take time from doing work to protect sacred places
in order to write about it.

Fortunately, there were writers and advocates who had time
and have written some gems. In separate essays, Ed Valandra and
Dan Wildcat brought to these pages our friend, the scholar–advocate
Vine Deloria Jr., Esq. (Standing Rock Sioux), in examining place and
vision. Rick Hill shares a Haudenosaunee context for considering
the sacred. In an oral history told to Tina Kuckkahn, Delbert Miller
leaves an important record of some things Skokomish elders say, and
Tina writes a lovely piece on one Anishinaabe sacred place. Attorney
Brett Shelton provides valuable ideas on things that Native Peoples,
collectively and individually, can do when trying to demonstrate in
court that they are the best stewards of the land. Gabrielle Tayac gives
us an information-rich piece on a Piscataway sacred place, the Potomac
River. Thank you all for these gifts and thank you, Lloyd, for your
guidance, patience and generosity. And special appreciation for our
peer reviewers. Respect for all.

For you, good reader, I leave a small reference gift. People always want to know what exactly is a sacred place. That often leads to
an interest in having a definition of one, something that all of us who
deal with this issue have resisted for several reasons: (1) no practitioners of other religions, ceremonies, cultures, or ways have to define the

sacred or spell out what a sacred place or object or context might be; (2) to define something is really to lose something, because no definition is all-encompassing; and (3) Native practitioners should not be held to a different standard—for all others, sacred is declaratory, it is sacred because those who are of that way hold it sacred. While the sacred should not be defined, it certainly can be explained. Here, for your reference, is an explanation we wrote when preparing the final report to Congress on the American Indian Religious Freedom Act:

> The Native peoples of this country believe that certain areas of land are holy. These lands may be sacred, for example, because of religious events which occurred there, because they contain specific natural products, because they are the dwelling place or embodiment of spiritual beings, because they surround or contain burial grounds or because they are sites conducive to communicating with spiritual beings. There are specific religious beliefs regarding each sacred site which form the basis for religious laws governing the site. These laws may prescribe, for example, when and for what purposes the site may or must be visited, what ceremonies or rituals may or must take place at the site, what manner of conduct must or must not be observed at the site, who may or may not go to the site and the consequences to the individual, group, clan or tribe if the laws are not observed. The ceremonies may also require preparatory rituals, purification rites or stages of preparation. Both active participants and observers may need to be readied. Natural substances may need to be gathered. Those who are unprepared or whose behavior or condition may alter the ceremony are often not permitted to attend. The proper spiritual atmosphere must be observed. Structures may need to be built for the ceremony or its preparation. The ceremony itself may be brief or it may last for days. The number of participants may range from one individual to a large group.

Suzan Shown Harjo (Cheyenne Citizen, Cheyenne & Arapaho Tribes, and Hotvlkvlke Mvskokvlke, Nuyakv) has been arguably the most consistent and effective advocate for Native American rights over the last six decades. She has served as president of the Morning Star Institute (1984-present) and former executive director of the National Congress of American Indians (1980s), Native American Rights Fund, Fried Frank legislative liaison, and Carter administration political appointee. In these roles, she has helped develop critical legislation, including the American Indian Religious Freedom Act of 1978 and AIRFA Amendments of 1994, the National Museum of the American Indian Act of 1989, the Native American Graves Protection and Repatriation Act of 1990 and the Eastern Land Acts of the Passamaquoddy Tribe, Penobscot Nation and the Mashantucket Pequot Tribal Nation (1980, 1984).

A founding trustee of the Smithsonian National Museum of the American Indian, columnist, curator, and poet, Harjo has been at the center of almost every legislative, legal, and cultural issue of import to Native Peoples, including protection of ancestors, children, cultural rights, land, water, and sacred places, as well as the return of more than one million acres of Indigenous lands. She had led successful campaigns to eliminate "Native" mascots and themes from American sports since the 1960s, including a quarter century of overlapping legal actions (1992–2009, 2006–17, 2010–17) against the R*dsk*ns name, which the Washington, DC, football team dropped in 2020. She also has been in the forefront of re-Indigenizing place-names, such as Piestewa Peak (2003, AZ; 2008, US Board on Geographic Names; from Sq**w), Little Bighorn Battlefield Monument Act (1990, from Custer), and Black Elk Peak (2016, from Harney).

A 2014 recipient of the Presidential Medal of Freedom, the United States' highest civilian honor, she is editor and guest curator of Nation to Nation: Treaties Between the United States and American Indian Nations, an award-winning exhibition (2014–2027, NMAI Museum on the Mall) and accompanying book (Smithsonian Books, 2014). She has received honorary doctorates from the Institute of American Indian Arts (Humanities, 2011) and Princeton University (Humane Letters, 2023). Inducted into the National Native American Hall of Fame for Advocacy (2022) and the Oklahoma Journalism Hall of Fame, she received the latter's Lifetime Achievement Award (2024). She is the first Native woman elected to both of the oldest learned societies in the United States: the American Academy of Arts and Sciences (Fellow, 2020) and the American Philosophical Society (Fellow, 2022).

Born in El Reno, Oklahoma, she was raised there in Cheyenne-Arapaho Treaty territory by her maternal grandparents, and on Muscogee allotted farmland on the Muscogee (Creek) Treaty Reservation by her paternal grandparents. She lived with her parents when they were stationed at Schofield Barracks, Oahu, Hawai'i; the Presidio at Monterey, California; and with Allied Forces Southern Europe, NATO, Napoli, Italia. As an adult, she has lived and worked in New York City, where she was a broadcast journalist, producer, and drama & literature director for WBAI-FM Radio, Pacifica Network's flagship free-speech station. In Santa Fe, New Mexico, she received unprecedented back-to-back residencies in poetry and as a 2004 summer scholar, and she served on the New Mexico Governor's Commission on Po'Pay to Statuary Hall, US Capitol. In Washington, DC, she started as news director for the American Indian Press Association, moved to advocacy, and returned to playwriting. Her poetry and other writings are widely anthologized; hundreds of her columns and articles have appeared in mainstream, tribal, and alternative media; and she has written for every version of *Indian Country Today*, from the original *Lakota Times* newspaper to the current online ICT.

In a Sacred Manner We Live
Haudenosaunee Reflections on Protecting the Sacred

Richard W. Hill

In July 2022 as I was watching the late Pope Francis visiting Lac Ste. Anne in Alberta, Canada, a place that many Catholic Indigenous believers hold sacred for its miraculous powers, I was struck by the devout faith exhibited by the attendees in relationship to that body of water. It was first referred to as Wakamne (translated by some Nakota to mean "God's Lake"). Local Cree speakers refer to it as Sakhahigan, or the Lake of the Spirit. When whites working for the Hudson's Bay Company arrived, they renamed it Devil's Lake. So it was ironic that now the pope was paying homage to the very same lake.

This scenario of renaming has played out across North America. What Indigenous peoples hold dear was often feared by the colonizing Christians. It was as if what we hold sacred was a manifestation of evil in their minds. The word *sacred* is a bit troubling in itself, as it often reflects the notion of religious veneration. For the purposes of this essay, I use *sacred* to mean an inherent spiritual power connected to events or places that still resonate within Indigenous belief systems.

There are old stories that a giant serpent named Jotéhkwatöh in the Seneca language once lived in the lake and was known to capsize a canoe or two by shaking its tail and causing dangerous waves and currents to form.[1] The Haudenosaunee have a similar story about such serpents in the Great Lakes and Niagara River corridor.

Somehow, the Catholic missionaries were able to transform Indigenous thinking toward the lake, and they started an annual pilgrimage to Lac Ste. Anne in 1889. Today, thousands travel to the lake, often barefoot, in hopes of a miracle. In 2004 the lake was declared a national historic site of social and cultural significance. The Parks Canada Agency explains the site as follows:

> Lac Ste. Anne Pilgrimage was designated a national historic site of Canada because: as early as 1889, Indigenous people, including Cree, Dene, Blackfoot and Métis, have been coming to Lac Ste. Anne to celebrate the Feast of Saint Anne. Saint Anne embodies, for many Indigenous people, the traditional importance of the grandmother figure; for the Indigenous people of Western and Northwestern Canada, it is an important place of social, cultural and spiritual rejuvenation, which are important aspects of the traditional summer gathering.[2]

Pope Francis visited the lake on the second day of his journey of reconciliation, seeking forgiveness for the crimes against humanity perpetrated by officials of the Catholic Church who operated Indian residential schools across Canada. The Truth and Reconciliation Commission of Canada, formed to document what happened in the residential schools, revealed the depth of abuse committed in the name of Jesus. The way things are going, it would take a miracle to undo the harm done. It was as if the residential schools became the physical manifestation of the evil underwater serpents, stalking Indigenous youth across the land, devouring their spirits as well as their bodies.

The history of Lac Ste. Anne forces us to ask, What makes something sacred to Indigenous Peoples? We often think of sacred landscapes as part of traditional Indigenous worldviews. The land is sacred because of its sacred origins and sacred intent. Lac Ste. Anne also forces us to consider what is sacred to colonized Indigenous Peoples, and should those sacred places receive the same level of protection and political reverence as older, traditional places of spirit?

As I traveled across Indian Country, I began to notice a shared tradition about water serpents expressed in story and visual art, everywhere from the dry Southwest to the lush green Midwest of the Mound Builders, the great expanse of water of the Great Lakes, the Appalachian Mountains of the Southeast, and beyond. Usually, the curvilinear body of the serpent mimics waves on the water, generally representing both life and its polar opposite.

Sometimes these serpents rise to the surface to signal tough times ahead; at times they shake their body in such a way as to easily upset a canoe and its human occupants, who quickly become the serpent's dinner. Other times, the serpent brings life-giving rains to replenish the soil, refresh the plants, and renew our life spirit.

Underwater creatures can be dangerous or benevolent; it is incumbent upon us to know the difference.

Among the Algonkian-speaking peoples of the Northeast and Great Lakes, a similar spirit is the Underwater Panther called Mishipeshu, which is visualized as a giant lynx with a long tail. Pictographs in Lake Superior Provincial Park in Ontario depict the Mishipeshu with horns on its head and a row of spikes down its spine. Today, some Anishinaabe elders say that the Mishipeshu serves to protect them and that they called upon it to help them defeat the Haudenosaunee by upsetting their canoes during the seventeenth-century Beaver Wars.

In Ohio we find an effigy mound that is likely a depiction of the underwater panther with a long tail. It was mistakenly labeled an alligator by archaeologists, but it clearly resembles a round-headed, four-footed creature with a long tail that circles around it. In Utah, a horned serpent pictograph can be found in the western San Rafael Swell. The Pueblo cultures of the Southwest often depict Awanyu—the horned or plumed serpent—on their ceramics. Awanyu is seen as the guardian of water and as responsible for bringing the precious rains. "The horned serpent continues to be revered as an important deity among the Pueblos and is known by various names among the different linguistic groups, including Kolowisi (Zuni), Paaloloqangw (Hopi), and Awanyu (Tewa)," according to archaeologist Polly Schaafsma.[3]

Tewa scholar Greg Cajete describes Indigenous peoples' deep connection to place as "Indian people expressed a relationship to the natural world that can only be called ensoulment." Cajete sees ensoulment as the most ancient foundation of human psychology. "The psychology and spiritual quality of Indian behavior, with its reflections in symbolism, were thoroughly 'informed' by the depth and power of their participation mystique and their perception of the Earth as a living soul."[4]

Thus, according to Cajete, relationships and responsibilities to place were solidified with the notion that spirit and matter are inseparable. Not only are we connected to place in profound ways, our children are also bestowed upon us through the earth, springs, lakes, mountains, or caves. People and places both shape each other, concludes Cajete. Sacred beings within a sacred landscape. Deeply connected. This inner kinship, as Cajete refers to it, produces our human psyche—a fact which explains the true nature of the disruption that comes from forced removal from ancestral places or from being denied access to the places that are portals to the spirit of life held within those places.[5]

Muscogee (Creek) storyteller Tony Mitchell Sr. shared a story about Owv Pohocvse'h (pronounced wee-wah-jah-zee), who was one of twin brothers. One brother was taken to the land to produce medicinal plants. The other brother, who was half snake, was taken to the lake to protect the waters. They would help each other from time to time. The Muscogee Creek believe that the water serpent lives in a whirlpool, sleeping at the bottom but awaiting unsuspecting boaters or swimmers that fall prey to its appetite.[6]

Back in my homelands of upstate New York, there are few places considered sufficiently sacred to be worthy of political and legal protection. We don't talk of the few that might be such because people will not understand and will likely try to exploit the sacredness of these sites. We simply continue to maintain a relationship with the spirit of that place. We have, however, shared information about some historically significant cultural/spirit places:

- **Place of Emergence.** Oral history tells of a place where our ancestors had been imprisoned underground and were released by the Creator to find places to settle and become nations.
- **Home of the Thunderbeings.** Oral history tells of the powerful spirits who once lived behind the mighty falls at Niagara. They are the ones responsible for bringing the dark clouds and loud thunder to chase away that underwater serpent I spoke of earlier.
- **Birthplace of the Peacemaker.** Oral history tells of the birth of the Peace Messenger who helped to create the Haudenosaunee Confederacy of the Five, later Six, Nations. This is the place where the Peacemaker made and launched a white stone canoe that carried him to the most evil people whose minds were converted to peace by the power of his spirit.
- **Tully Lakes.** Oral tradition tells us that Hyenwatha, the Peacemaker's assistant, discovered tubular shell wampum beads on the lakebed after a flock of ducks lifted all the water from the lake into the air. Those beads helped to relieve grief-stricken minds so that peace would become possible.
- **Lake Onondaga.** Oral tradition informs us this is the place where the Peacemaker brought good-minded leaders in a flotilla of canoes to confront and pacify the most powerful Onondaga wizard, named Tadodaho, thereby making the Great Law of Peace possible.
- **Onondaga Fire Keepers.** The Grand Council of the Haudenosaunee meets in the territory of the Onondaga Nation, and the place where the council fire is kindled is considered sacred. It is a protected place, and as the smoke rises straight upward, it signals to other nations that that the Great Law continues to this very day. This

is more like a sacred event in which the intention of the
Creator is made visible.

Whenever the Haudenosaunee gather, be it for political, spiritual, cultural, or social events, a great expression of gratitude is offered.
Known as the Words Before All Others, this is basically a recounting
of what is sacred in the Haudenosaunee universe. It goes well beyond
place and mixes evidence of natural phenomena with conceptual spiritual forces that combine to keep life going. The Short Mohawk Version
of the Thanksgiving, includes the following elements:

> **ONKWEHSHON:A (The People).** May we now gather
> our minds as one and give one another greetings and
> thanks that we are gathered here in good health and in
> peace. (All agree.)
>
> **IETHINISTENHA ONHWENTSIA (Mother Earth).** May we
> now gather our minds together as one and greet and
> give our thanks to our Mother Earth for all that she
> gives us so we may live.
>
> **OHNEKASHON:A (The Water).** May we now gather our
> minds together as one and turn to the spirit of the wa-
> ters of the world; with oneness of mind, we now send
> our thanks to the waters of the world for quenching our
> thirst and purifying our lives.
>
> **KARIOTA'SHON:'A (Animal Life).** May we now gather
> our minds as one and give our words of greetings and
> thanks to the animals.
>
> **OKWIRE'SHON:'A (Trees of the Forest).** May we now
> gather our minds together as one and give greetings and
> thanks to the trees of the forest for the fruits we eat, for
> the shade in summer, and for the shelter of our homes.
>
> **OTSI'TEN'OKON:'A (Bird Life).** The Creator instructed the
> birds to sing upon the arrival of each new day, and to
> sing so that all life will not know boredom. With one
> mind we now greet and thank the bird life.
>
> **RATIWE:RAS (Grandfather Thunders).** The Creator in-
> structed the Grandfather Thunders to put fresh water
> in the rivers, lakes, and springs to quench the thirst of
> life. So with one mind we give our greetings and thanks
> to our grandfathers.
>
> **EHTSITEWAHTSI:'A KIEHKEHNEKHA KARAHKWA (Our Eldest
> Brother, The Sun).** We are the younger siblings, and our
> Brother Sun shines the light so we may see and radiates
> warmth that all life may grow. We now with one mind
> give greetings and thanks to our Eldest Brother, The Sun.

IETHIHSOTHA AHSONTHENHKA KARAHKWA (**Our Grandmother, The Moon**). Our Creator placed her in charge of the birth of all things and made her leader of all female life. All babies of all nations are born by her orchestration. May we now gather our minds into one and send our greetings and our thanksgiving to our Grandmother, The Moon.

SHONKWAIA'TISON (**Our Creator**). Our Creator made all of life with nothing lacking. All we humans are required to do is waste no life and be grateful daily to all life. And so now we gather all our minds into one and send our greetings and our thanksgiving to our maker, our Creator.

This oral tradition links all the preceding elements in a sacred relationship to each other. Take humans as an example. The first humans were made from the clay of the Mohawk Earth. The Creator breathed his sacred breath into those figures so that they could become animated and could walk about, see, feel, sense, and think. This was done so that they could comprehend the beautiful nature of this world, which provides all that is needed to be healthy and well fed. In this regard, even food is sacred because it provides the fuel for our sacred bodies and reinforces our sacred relationship to the created world.

Humans are asked to accept on faith that the celestial bodies also contribute to that completeness. The sun, moon, stars, and winds provide tangible benefits, but we take it on faith that they have a spiritual essence we can communicate with. They provide assistance, but that assistance depends upon our conduct and our faith in them. Actually, we can see the power of their actions, so this is more than a matter of faith, it is Indigenous science—the predictable outcomes of natural phenomena and cultural practices. Time-tested and true.

Yet, there are also spiritual forces that we cannot see. Our cultural worldview and oral history explain that intangible spirits also influence our lives and are affected by our words, thoughts, and actions. Our relationship with these forces is a codependency in the most powerful of ways. Our Haudenosaunee culture also explains that our ancestors and recently departed relatives also have spiritual energy. This is why we are so particular about how our relatives are buried and are even more adamant that they should not be disturbed after their burial. They still have responsibilities to fulfill. They still have spiritual energy. They still shape the quality of our lives.

Tuscarora scholar J. N. B Hewitt, working at the Bureau of American Ethnology in the late nineteenth and early twentieth centuries, wrote about the dual nature of our souls. Hewitt stated that when we no longer have breath, part of our "Mind" soul, which gave us our individual character, departs the body and makes its journey back to the land of souls in the Sky World. Eventually, that mind soul will be sent back to the earth to animate the thinking of a newborn baby. Hewitt also spoke of a "Bone" soul that rests within the very bones of the human body. That soul mixes with the soil of the burial and gives energy to help plants grow, blossom, and mature. In this regard, all soil is the result of our decomposing bodies combining with the decomposition of all living things to create new earth.[7]

Niagara Falls has been identified by both the Iroquoian-speaking and Algonkian-speaking cultures as a special place because of the spirits that once inhabited the caves behind the falls. Niagara Falls was one of the legendary stops along the Great Anishinaabe Migration from the Atlantic coast to the upper Great Lakes. At Niagara, the Anishinaabe ancestors became acquainted with the power Thunderbirds who use their lightning bolts to control the behaviors of an underwater serpent/panther. This is why you will often see decorated pouches or textiles that have a Thunderbird on one side and the Underwater Panther on the other. Humans exist between those two realms and can be affected by both.

For the Haudenosaunee, our oral history speaks of Thunder Beings that lived in a large cave behind Niagara Falls, who had a similar responsibility of chasing down and destroying horned serpents living within the deep waterways. The stories tell of two kinds of serpents: one that could be beneficial to humans and one that seeks our destruction. The dangerous serpents will attack people on or near water but are also responsible for poisoning the water in the springs and headwaters on which we depend. The Thunder Beings use their arrows, which turn into lightning bolts, to kill the serpents before they reach those sources of freshwater. The dangerous serpents are also said to stalk humans, bringing famine and diseases to our ancestral communities. As I look upon the beautiful sunlight dancing upon Lake Erie or Lake Ontario, I often think of what lies beneath the surface.

History has taught us to make sure we have the right relationship with the earth, the water, and the spirits of place in order to ensure our survival. In our Creation Story, the Creator picked up a handful of soil and said, "This is alive." Soil was made before the Creator walked the earth, but he set in motion a spiritually based cultural practice that reenergizes the soil and ensures that life here on earth continues as intended.

So, how do you pull one part out of that interconnected web of life and say that it is more important than the others? How do you say some parts are more sacred than others? In many ways for the Haudenosaunee, and I believe, for most Indigenous cultures, sacredness is a state of mind that transcends place. "Place" can kick-start a whole series of relationships and responsibilities, but what makes that place significant is the power of belief, belief in the intangible, belief that somehow this all makes sense. As I saw the pope and the Catholic faithful gather at Lac Ste. Anne, I was thinking about the power of belief combined with the power of place.

At a small settlement in Mohawk Country, the National Shrine of the North American Martyrs sits in a place named Auriesville, near the seventeenth-century Mohawk village of Ossernenon. At this location the Mohawks executed three Jesuits: Rene Goupil, John LaLande, and Father Isaac Joques. They were later canonized as saints by the Catholic Church. The place is very sacred to devout believers. It is their belief that empowers this place.

If eyewitness accounts and history books are to be believed, the Mohawks were quite severe in their treatment of Joques. He was tortured and eventually executed, being held to blame for a host of problems that arrived in Mohawk Country with the entrance of the Black Robes. More than half the population of the Mohawk Nation died from European diseases carried by the Jesuits and fur traders. Were the Black Robes manifestations of the life-devouring serpent? In Haudenosaunee tradition, a place associated with massive bloodspilling becomes a place to be avoided, not commemorated. The Mohawks would let the earth renew itself at that place, in the hope that, eventually, the spirit of the Mother Earth would dissipate the bloodstains and recover its original sacredness.

As I drive throughout our homelands, I reflect on my efforts to recover the remains of our ancestors that have been uncovered by archaeologists, bulldozer operators, and farmers on their tractors. Those ancestors have taught me that the bone souls of those who came before me are everywhere, not just where their bodies were buried. The earth vibrates with their spiritual energy. The dead have a whole network of bone souls at work every day; they gather underground, combine their energies, and continue to work for our benefit. Every now and then, they send one of their company upward to reveal their bones, just as a reminder to us that everywhere we go, sacredness surrounds us. It is a great act of love. We need to return the gesture by loving this place so much that we will not destroy it for another casino, another shopping mall, or another pipeline. Doing so requires that we live more humbly in relationship to the sacredness in which we have been placed. By living in a sacred manner, the Creation folds out as intended and gives us the ability to navigate around the dark forces that also exist within Creation. In our worldview, it was the Creator's intent that we use the power of our minds to make conscious choices to follow the sacred path laid out before us. If we do so, we enhance both ourselves and the places of energy that exist within the sacred landscape of our Mother Earth.

Rick Hill (Tuscarora Nation, Beaver Clan) is a writer, curator, and artist. He previously served as museum director at the Institute of American Indian Arts, Santa Fe, New Mexico; as assistant director for public programs at the National Museum of the American Indian; and as a faculty member in Native American Studies at the University of Buffalo.

NOTES

1 Arthur Caswell Parker, *Seneca Myths and Folk Tales* (Buffalo, NY: Buffalo Historical Society, 1923); Jeremiah Curtin and J. N. B. Hewitt, *Seneca Indian Myths* (New York: E. P. Dutton, 1923).

2 Lac Ste. Anne Pilgrimage National Historic Site of Canada, Parks Canada, https://www.pc.gc .ca/apps/dfhd/page_nhs_eng.aspx ?id=10273.

3 RoseMary Diaz, "Avanyu: Spirit of Water in Pueblo Life and Art," *Santa Fe New Mexican*, May 14, 2014.

4 Gregory Cajete, *Native Science— Natural Laws of Interdependence* (Santa Fe, NM: Clear Light, 2000), 186.

5 Gregory Cajete, "Ensoulment of Nature," in *Native Heritage, Personal Accounts by American Indians, 1790 to Present*, ed. Arlene Hirschfelder (New York: Macmillan), 1995.

6 Deborah Mitchell, "King of the Waters: The Legend of the Horned Water Serpent," 1997 Native American Symposium, Native American Institute, Southeastern Oklahoma State University, https://www.se.edu /native-american/wp-content /uploads/sites/49/2019/09/2nd symposiumpart5.pdf.

7 J. N. B. Hewitt, "The Iroquoian Concept of the Soul," *Journal of American Folklore* 8, no. 29 (1895): 107–16.

In the Presence of the Secular
Protecting Sacred Places

Waŋblí Wapȟáha Hokšíla (Edward Valandra)

> Sacred places are the foundation of all other
> beliefs and practices because they represent
> the presence of the sacred in our lives. . . . We
> can hope that some protection can be afforded
> [to] these sacred places before the world be-
> comes wholly secular and is destroyed.
> —*Vine Deloria Jr.*, God Is Red

SETTLER PROLEGOMENA

In 1985, Imre Sutton, a white settler, edited *Irredeemable America*, a book about Indigenous land claims (through the Indian Claims Commission) against the US settler state.[1] He wrote a prolegomenon to explain, among other things, settler ambivalence toward these land claims.[2] Despite this ambivalence, he reassured fellow settlers that they need not fear their worst nightmare—an Indigenous eviction notice from their ill-gotten land.

> Tribes everywhere have neither enough land nor sufficient
> good land, but, as readers will soon realize, the outcome
> of land-claims litigation has not turned on the restoration
> of land. At no time has Irredeemable America been in
> jeopardy. *The title to the American continent remains securely in the*
> *hands of the White majority.*[3]

In 1984, white settler Ronald Reagan launched his political ad *Morning in America*, which soothed white fears about an uncertain racial future; a year later, Sutton was telling settlers they had little to fear from Indigenous Peoples. He reminded them that America is, after all, *irredeemable*. Furthermore, though he describes Indigenous Peoples as embittered over being dispossessed of our land, he affirms that we have no choice but to accept this injustice—this crime against our humanity.

> Wrongful deeds perpetrated on the tribes by avaricious citizens and reproachable officials only remind Indians of this continuum of events that has unceasingly pitted tribes against non-Indians. Moreover, the tribes have been embittered by having to acknowledge that their title to such lands has been forever extinguished whenever they have accepted judgment funds. *If Indians continue to be aggrieved over the wrongful taking of land*, it is not just because so little land has ever been regained, but because the litigation process—once perceived as their only recourse—has not fully met their expectations of an honorable resolution. The point is, Indians do not want money; they want land. *We must face the fact that land is something that whites are always unwilling to give them.*[4]

Settlers' pattern of land theft is either to forcibly remove us from our national territories or to reduce our homelands to reservations/reserves in severalty—that is, through allotment. Consequently, most significant landmarks or sites and cultural areas known as sacred now exist outside our reservations/reserves. These sacred places have become part of illegally annexed Indigenous lands, which are settler-designated as either public domain or private lands. While these "off-reservation" places remain sacred to us, Indigenous-led political challenges to adverse settler court and administrative decisions and institutional policies have shown that our access to these sacred places for spiritual or cultural activities has proven difficult, if not prohibited. Indeed, settler governments, organizations, and most individual settlers make little to no effort to protect Indigenous sacred places from development and other harmful settler practices that desecrate them.

Settlers remain intransigent against returning stolen Indigenous land. Yet, at least two developments are challenging their intransigence: the increasing number of Indigenous Land Acknowledgment (ILA) statements across North America and the growing shift from retributive justice to the use of reparative/restorative justice or restorative practices. Rather than focusing on which laws have been broken, who the lawbreaker is, and what their "deserved" punishment is, non-retributive justice focuses on repairing or undoing harm resulting from wrongdoing. Indeed, the intersection of ILAs and reparative justice points to protecting sacred places; that is, it opens a pathway toward making amends and putting things right.

The ILA practice shows that, compared to the last century, settlers are more aware of legacy harms, such as the residential school system, visited upon Indigenous Peoples. For instance, on June 11, 2008, Canadian Prime Minister Stephen Harper read, with noticeable discomfort, a public, televised apology to Indigenous Peoples for residential school harms. From 2008 to 2015, Canada's Truth and Reconciliation Commission (TRC) conducted a residential school investigation that raised troubling questions about settler behavior and attitudes toward Indigenous Peoples. ILAs also raise deep moral and ethical questions for settlers. Some of these questions have led to critiques of ILAs. Thanks to these critiques, ILAs are shifting from the performative to calls for action. No doubt, ILAs have emerged as a common Canadian practice that is only beginning to spread to their settler cousins in the United States.

Moreover, because the criminal justice systems in both Canada and the United States are doing what they were designed for—criminalizing Indigenous Peoples, people of color, and other marginalized communities—the justice system and its ancillaries (for example, school-to-prison pipeline) carry on the systemic violence and structural harms directed at Indigenous Peoples and people of color. Comparatively, we are overrepresented in the prison-industrial complex and, as nonwhites, we are highly subject to being surveilled. Conversely, the Black Lives Matter movement, the Missing and Murdered Indigenous Women & Girls movement, the Abolitionist movement, the climate change movement, and other community movements aim to dismantle systemic violence and its structural harms. Hence, restorative/reparative justice, restorative practices, and other forms of non-retributive justice have emerged as grassroots participants organize alternatives to retributive justice.

Until recently, non-retributive approaches have been limited to individuals. In a nutshell, an individual did the harm, another individual was at the receiving end of that harm, and the harm was repaired person-to-person. However, the community movements show that restorative/reparative justice and similar movements have not addressed or dealt with systemic or structural harm. For instance, settlers Andrew Woolford and Amanda Nelund discuss the political nature of restorative justice, which has implications for reparative justice. A substantive critique is that restorative/reparative justice, when limited to individual applications, fails to address the structural harms that cause lethal and ongoing harm to entire populations.

If restorative justice does not avoid the narrowing defi-
nitions of criminal law, it is likely to remain silent with
respect to serious injustices that threaten to cause a
great deal of harm. . . . One of the most troubling cases
of environmental damage has occurred in the village of
Fort Chipewyan . . . where doctors have confirmed the
Indigenous population suffers from a higher than expected rate of cancer, including rare bile-duct cancers.
Fort Chipewyan rests on the shores of Lake Athabasca,
which is fed by the Athabasca River and has been found
to contain unsafe levels of arsenic, mercury, and poly-
cyclic aromatic hydrocarbon. While there is not yet
absolute proof the problems faced in this community are
the result of the conversion of the Tar Sands' bitumen into
crude oil, processing this crude oil does produce large
amounts of contaminated water, all of which may not be
properly contained.

Does restorative justice not have a place in such a
conflict? A restorative justice that sought to be a significant alternative to the formal criminal justice system,
especially one geared toward transformative ends, would
need to address such potentially disastrous injustices,
given their terrible toll on human lives, even (or especially)
if the law has not yet seen fit to criminalize them.[5]

If restorative justice can be called on to address and undo structural violence and harm, then reparative justice, as Woolford and
Nelund argue, would necessarily involve protecting sacred places.
This call for reparative justice to do some heavy lifting is timely. After
all, ILAs have been raising both deep moral and discomforting ethical questions for several years; reparative justice, which is now raising
questions of morality and ethics as well, becomes a critically important framework for Indigenous Peoples and settler–perpetrators to talk
about protecting sacred places.

INDIGENOUS LAND
ACKNOWLEDGMENT:
REVISITING IRREDEEMABILITY

When Covid-19 achieved pandemic status in the United States, online
virtual gatherings replaced in-person gatherings. I participated in numerous online restorative justice and restorative practices gatherings
in the United States, and sometimes settlers from Canada attended
these gatherings as well. It struck me that almost all of them did not
open with an ILA. At times, I pointed out to the settler participants

attending these virtual gatherings that their settler cousins in Canada routinely open with such a statement in public spaces. In response to my observation, some settlers remarked that they "felt unsure" about opening with an ILA and did not know how one is done "properly." In these online spaces, normative settler behaviors reveal that they do not know the names of the Indigenous Peoples or Nations whose land they are illegally occupying. Even when they offer ILAs, they seldom acknowledge lands that Indigenous Nations acknowledge as sacred, nor do they acknowledge the harm that settlers have done to these lands.

Before discussing how decolonized ILAs may yet contribute to protecting places we know to be sacred, we must consider protocols. A proper protocol concerns the question, "Where are you from?" For Indigenous Peoples, there is both a within-nation and out-of-nation protocol. For my people (within-nation), the protocol consists of all or most of the following: a traditional greeting that acknowledges the people as relatives and identifies who you are. Who you are consists of knowing your *thióšpaye;* the *oyáŋke* you traditionally come from; who your parents and grandparents are; the *oyáŋke pi* they traditionally come from; which *thióšpaye* they come from; your *óšpáye;* and which *Očhéthi Šakówiŋ* you come from or identify with. I have also been privileged to be in other Indigenous Peoples' territories, and I have witnessed similar protocols but unique to their nation. When visiting other Indigenous Peoples' territories (out-of-nation), we follow at minimum four protocol rules: we acknowledge ourselves as guests and say how we came into their territory; how we will honor their ways; and how we will do no harm, just as a relative would not do.

For Indigenous Peoples, our customary protocols embed unspoken ILAs. Yet, such customary protocols are frightening—if not unsettling—for settlers. For one, they restate a hard-to-refute truth: that our mere physical presence in North America undoes the elaborate, settler-constructed fiction of them laying "claim" to our homelands. For another, US settlers' birther movement has weaponized asking someone, "Where you from?" Depending on the settler's immigration status and other social variables, the response varies. A settler immigrant who is white and born in the United States assumes that nonwhite settler immigrants, even those born in the United States like Barack Hussein Obama II, are suspect, not entitled to the protections, privileges, and immunities of a "legitimate settler."

Notwithstanding Indigenous customary ILA protocols, ILA statements originated in Canada and are very recent in the United States. Before 1973, the Canadian settler-state did not acknowledge; that is, recognize, Indigenous land titles of any kind. On 31 January 31, 1973, however, the settlers' highest court in Canada ruled, for the first time, in *Calder et al. v. Attorney General of British Columbia,* that an aboriginal title does exist.[6] Since *Calder,* aboriginal title has been the focus of much Canadian settler litigation, policies, declarations, laws, social justice organizations, academic articles, and op-ed pieces. Indigenous Peoples, of course, oppose or challenge the settler colonialism inherent in all these mechanisms/political devices/media. For example, after *Calder*, the following Indigenous realities pushed Canada's political developments to refine settler relations with Indigenous Peoples, and the public practice of ILAs has been one outcome:

- In patriating its constitution in 1982, Canada also adopted the Charter of Rights and Freedoms. Both instruments—the constitution and the charter—recognized aboriginal peoples' existing treaty rights.
- Other settler court decisions, such as *R. v. Sparrow* (1990) and *Delgamuukw v. British Columbia* (1997), further clarified Section 35 of the constitution, which affirms existing aboriginal and treaty rights.
- In 1991, the Royal Commission on Aboriginal Peoples (RCAP) examined aboriginal peoples' status and rights and the relationship between Indigenous Peoples and Canadian settler society. The RCAP published its four-thousand-page report in 1996.
- Canada established the TRC (2008–15) to address the residential school system's abuse of Indigenous children as genocide against Indigenous Peoples.
- Canada eventually adopted the UN General Assembly's Declaration on the Rights of Indigenous Peoples (UNDRIP, June 21, 2021, Bill C-15) after initially rejecting it (along with Australia, New Zealand, and the United States) in a General Assembly vote (September 13, 2007).

In 2004, thirty years after *Calder* but before the TRC and UNDRIP, Michael Asch, a white Canadian settler, deconstructed *Calder*'s implications. On the one hand, the settler narrative long held that, because of Indigenous Peoples' "primitive state," the Crown, and later Canada, felt no need whatsoever to recognize or acknowledge Indigenous sovereignty; that is, outright land title (ownership). On the other hand, in *Calder*, the Canadian settler Supreme Court rejected these presumptions or interpretations about Indigenous Peoples' primitiveness, which lower courts have used to dismiss Indigenous land claims.

Given that the [Chief Justice] Davey representation [Indigenous society = primitiveness] is deeply offensive to contemporary understandings espoused in U.N.

declarations and [Justice Emmett M.] Hall's judgment
[Indigenous society = developed], it is hard to understand . . . why post-Calder jurisprudence does not simply
reject it [the Davey representation]. There are many expla-
nations, but one goes to the heart of the lesson in Calder:
To adopt that judgment's representation [i.e., Hall's] would
represent a challenge to the political tenets that explain
the legitimacy of the Canadian state so sweeping that the
court could not dare to adopt the judgement without public or government support.[7]

In addition to these Indigenous realities, Asch squarely outlined/
named what *Calder* means for settler occupation of our homelands,
whether in Canada or the United States.

Again, Canada still rests its foundational political legitimacy on the ideology and legal reasoning of English colonialism. The lynch pin of this ideology and legal regime
is the firm conviction that the acquisition of sovereignty,
legislative authority, and underlying title by the Crown is
not problematic even without the assent of the indigenous
peoples on whose territories Canadians settled. Were the
court to adopt the representation of indigenous society
advanced in Calder, it would, by necessity, invalidate this
assumption. *Under such conditions, the legitimacy of Canadians'
claim to sovereignty, legislative authority, and underlying title without the express consent of indigenous peoples is called into question.*
These are dangerous grounds for the judiciary to occupy,
both in terms of audacity and of its capacity as a creature
of the state within which it is embedded.
    The courts, then, face a dilemma of the first order.
On one hand, it is unconscionable to continue representing indigenous peoples in terms that are demeaning and
offensive to contemporary understandings and values.
On the other, were the courts to fully adopt the Calder
representation, they would change the foundations of the
Canadian political order. Therefore, the judiciary will not
make this change on its own.[8]

By 2004, *Calder* had seeded the ILA movement without the settlers in North America realizing it. Furthermore, events like the failed
1987 Meech Lake Constitutional Accord, the 1991 Oka Crisis, other
Indigenous-led self-determination actions, and the TRC provided the
rain and the soil for the ILA movement to grow and spread, eventually
reaching a justice-starved, albeit anti-Indigenous, US settler society.[9]

The June 11, 2008, apology from Canada's white prime minister on behalf of settlers for their extremely abusive residential school system and the TRC's work awakened settler Canada. The TRC heard testimony from residential school survivors and released several TRC volumes. TRC volume 6 dealt with reconciliation and mentioned "land" at least ninety-five times. For Canadian and later US settlers, then, ILAs, though not officially sanctioned or mandated, have become a socially acceptable way to "admit" how they have wronged and harmed Indigenous Peoples, while still benefiting from settler colonialism.

CRITICISMS OF ILAs: WHERE IS THE MORAL CENTER?

By 2017, Stephen Marche, a Canadian settler, noted that ILA statements were so mainstreamed that they were read even before hockey games, their national sport:

> I hear the same little speech, or a version of it, at gala
> events—literary prizes, political fundraisers, that sort
> of thing—when whichever government representative
> happens to be there reads some kind of acknowledgment
> before his or her introductory remarks. But you know
> a phenomenon has really arrived in Canada when it in-
> volves hockey. Both the Winnipeg Jets and the Edmonton
> Oilers began acknowledging traditional lands in their
> announcements before all home games last season.
> Acknowledgment is beginning to emerge as a kind of acci-
> dental pledge of allegiance for Canada—a statement made
> before any undertaking with a nation.[10]

To the uninitiated, ILAs appear to be a good thing. After all, they "acknowledge" the Indigenous inhabitants whose land settlers still illegally live, work, and play on. For example, at the Society for Cinema and Media Studies (SCMS) Fifty-Ninth Annual Conference, which was held in Toronto, Ontario, in 2018, the panel chairs were asked to read the following sixty-eight-word land acknowledgment statement aloud at the beginning of each session.

> To begin, we wish to acknowledge this land on which the
> SCMS conference is taking place. For thousands of years
> it has been the traditional land of the Huron-Wendat, the
> Seneca, and, most recently, the Mississaugas of the Credit
> River. Today this meeting place is still the home to many
> Indigenous people from across Turtle Island, and we are
> grateful to have the opportunity to work on this land.[11]

SCMS' ILA represents, of course, just one of many versions used throughout Canada. Marche discusses how the following eighty-one-word ILA said aloud where his children attend school is problematic:

> I would like to acknowledge that this school is situ-
> ated upon traditional territories. The territories include
> the Wendat, Anishinabek Nation, the Haudenosaunee
> Confederacy, the Mississaugas of the New Credit First
> Nations, and the Metis Nation. The treaty that was signed
> for this particular parcel of land is collectively referred
> to as the Toronto Purchase and applies to lands east of
> Brown's Line to Woodbine Avenue and north towards
> Newmarket. I also recognize the enduring presence of
> Aboriginal peoples on this land.[12]

Other ILAs do much the same. For Marche, settler-led ILAs become, among other things, mired in the acknowledgment's wording and meaning. For example, Marche asks readers to consider what "traditional" lands or territories mean. "Does it simply mean 'not legal'? Does it mean 'sort of but not really'? Whose tradition are we referring to?" Settlers in both Canada and the United States must ponder these core questions if they ever hope to reconcile their theft—and therefore illegal occupation—of Indigenous lands. Land theft and occupation are first among the genocidal harms that Indigenous Peoples have experienced at the hands of settlers.

Perhaps the most disturbing aspect of ILAs is that they fail to move settlers to action—to right wrongs that involve the most basic of human rights. Again, Marche casts a critical eye at ILAs because, while they say so much, they mean and do so little for colonized Indigenous Peoples:

> At bottom of the acknowledgment, unintentionally, are
> essential human questions of ethics and the ephemeral-
> ity of all history and what it means to live on the earth.
> Whenever I hear the acknowledgment read out loud, it
> provokes strongly conflicted feelings in me. It reveals to
> me the sinking burden of my own ignorance—who are
> the Wendat? It reveals the gap between intention and ac-
> tion in my country—seeing a lieutenant governor read the
> acknowledgment out loud is a living allegory of Canada's
> striving absurdity. But, the more often I hear acknowledg-
> ments, the more I hate how they're written—the passive
> constructions, the useless adverbs, the Latinate jargon,
> and, in the case of the acknowledgment at my children's
> school, that last sentence, about the continued presence

of indigenous peoples on the land, comes as pure after-
thought. They are written, it seems to me, so that we may
express a sentiment without, as far as possible, feeling it,
a natural result of being written by academic committees
and government lawyers. They sound like microwave warranties, not the desire for atonement.[13]

Perhaps it is not fair to compare ILAs with appliance warranties. After all, written warranties at least ensure a modicum of consumer protection in which an appliance can be returned or exchanged; ILAs offer no such protection or guarantees. Indeed, if ILAs were equivalent to warranties, then the settler institutions and organizations that issue ILAs should be sued for misrepresenting themselves to the public, implying something they do not intend to deliver.

Therein lies the rub.

For instance, Marche notes that, though sanitized, settlers' ILAs force them "to ask a basic, nightmarish question: Whose land are we on?" Indeed, the SCMS's explanation of its ILA—Why recognize land?—to its attendees expresses an unspoken discomfort underlying ILAs.

To recognize the land is an expression of gratitude and
appreciation to those whose territory you reside on, and
a way of honoring the Indigenous people who have been
living and working on the land from time immemorial. It
is important to understand the longstanding history that
has brought you to reside on the land, and to seek to understand your place within that history. Land acknowledgments do not exist in the past tense, or outside historical
context: colonialism is an ongoing process, and we need to
build our mindfulness of our present participation.[14]

Inserting colonialism (that is, settler colonialism) into ILA's "expression of gratitude and appreciation" or "way of honoring the Indigenous people" raises the ante. It strips away the warm fuzzy feelings that ILAs engender in settlers. How can Indigenous Peoples receive such gratitude or honor when ILAs present an illusion of civil relations between nations and peoples that does not align with our experiences as Indigenous Peoples? The reality is that settlers have committed mass crimes against us and are continuing to benefit from them but are not acknowledging these crimes in their ILAs. Fortunately, Asch and Marche challenged their settler readers about Canada's settler character, raising emotionally uncomfortable conversations about the settlers' presence in North America. Not surprisingly, US-colonized Indigenous Peoples, among others, also take aim at ILAs while settlers stare figuratively at their navels.

Elisa J. Sobo (settler), Michael Lambert (Cherokee citizen), and Valerie Lambert (Choctaw citizen) also question the value of settler-sanctioned ILAs, even those that involve Indigenous input. They argue that, in their current state, ILAs do more harm to Indigenous Peoples than good, which is not what ILAs are supposed to do.

> No data exist to demonstrate that land acknowledgments lead to measurable, concrete change. . . . Take, for instance, the evocation in many acknowledgments of a time when Indigenous peoples acted as "stewards" or "custodians" of the land now occupied. This and related references—for example, to "ancestral homelands"—relegate Indigenous peoples to a mythic past and fails to acknowledge that they owned the land. Even if unintentionally, such assertions tacitly affirm the putative right of non-Indigenous people to now claim title.
>
> This [settler "title claim"] is also implied in what goes unsaid: After acknowledging that an institution sits on another's land, there is no follow-up. Plans are almost never articulated to give the land back. This implication is: "What was once yours is now ours."
>
> Additionally, in most cases these statements fail to acknowledge the violent trauma of land being stolen from Indigenous people—the death, dispossession and displacement of countless individuals and much collective suffering. The afterlives of these traumas are deeply felt and experienced in Indigenous communities.[15]

By describing settlers' "rightful" claim to our respective homelands as putative, Sobo and the Lamberts unsettle settlers—as they should. For example, the 1868 Fort Laramie Treaty between my people and US settlers made explicit that, other than US personnel so authorized, our homeland is off-limits to settlers.

> [T]he United States now solemnly agrees that no persons except those herein designated and authorized so to do, and except such officers, agents, and employees of the Government as may be authorized to enter upon Indian reservations in discharge of duties enjoined by law, *shall ever be permitted to pass over, settle upon, or reside in the territory described in this article*, or in such territory as may be added to this reservation for the use of said Indians.[16]

What, then, do today's settlers, who freely "pass over, settle upon, or reside" within the exterior boundaries of my homeland, make of the fact that it is illegal for them to do so? As Asch noted, they have never obtained our consent, which the treaty requires. Because settlers continue to violate this treaty provision, they are technically undocumented immigrants. But more than that, their uninvited presence speaks volumes about the settler-induced traumas and violence that my people, as well as other Indigenous Peoples in North America, have experienced and continue to experience.

While settlers recite ILAs ad nauseam in the hope that these recitals may lead to reconciliation, Marche is highly skeptical—and for good reason.

> The idea behind the Canadian [or US] acknowledgment is that if we repeat the truth often enough, publicly enough, to children who are young enough, it will lead us to reconciliation. I might even agree, if not for Muskrat Falls. In the autumn after the principal started reading the acknowledgments at my children's school, leaders of the Inuit, the Nunatsiavut, and the NunatuKavut near Muskrat Falls, in Labrador, went on hunger strikes to protest the construction of a hydroelectric dam on their traditional territories. The rising mercury levels in the water because of the dam meant that the food supply of the territory, and the cultural practices that relied on fish and seal, would be disrupted.
>
> To me, Muskrat Falls re-created the whole of the Canadian colonial project, with all of its evils, in miniature. The Truth and Reconciliation Commission report of 2015 described Canadian colonization as a conquest with two major thrusts: the starvation of indigenous groups, and the attempt to erase indigenous languages and religious practices. In Muskrat Falls, it was happening all over again— disrupting food and culture. . . . The hypocrisy of the country can be so startling exactly because we repeat our good intentions so insistently. We say, over and over, that we want desperately to atone for a crime while we're still in the middle of committing it.[17]

Moreover, as Asch, Sobo, the Lamberts, and so many others like them recognize, the realities of Muskrat Falls do not find their way into contemporary ILAs—and that is no mere oversight either.

Other egregious ILA practices involve settlers finding an individual who is a citizen of an Indigenous Nation—or failing that, a "pretendian"—who is willing to perform a blessing ritual of some kind to accompany an ILA recital. For Sobo, the Lamberts, and Indigenous Peoples, these Hollywood-like performances attack our sovereignty at best and ensure our erasure as self-determining peoples at worse:

American Indian identity is a political identity based
on citizenship in an Indigenous nation whose sovereignty has been acknowledged by the U.S. government.
Sovereign Indigenous nations, and only these nations,
have the authority to determine who is and is not a citizen, and hence who is and is not an American Indian or
Alaska Native. . . . And so, particularly when they per-
petuate misunderstandings of Indigenous identities, land
acknowledgments done wrong are heard by Indigenous
peoples as the final blow: a definitive apocalyptic vision of
a world in which Indigenous sovereignty and land rights
will not be recognized and will be claimed never to have
really existed.[18]

Of course, Marche and his ilk raise a very difficult question about
settler ILAs: Can ILAs coexist with ongoing settler-perpetuated harms
across North America and have any shred of authenticity? The answer
is, "Of course not!" More importantly, can ILAs do the heavy lifting
required to make things right between Indigenous Peoples and settlers? Evidence shows that ILAs seemingly obscure the Muskrat Falls
transpiring throughout North America. Sobo and the Lamberts charge
that ILAs have failed to morally move settlers and their institutions
to any meaningful reparative justice. Instead, they maintain settler
colonialism—the status quo. I agree.

REPARATIVE JUSTICE: DISMANTLING IRREDEEMABILITY

Despite ILAs' shortcomings, they nonetheless persist as performative
nods to "doing the right thing." For example, in *Yellowstone*, a popular
TV series about modern-day settlers, season one's first episode shows
uneasy settlers living next to Indigenous Peoples. An exchange between a white settler—a proverbial wannabe Indian—and his young
son (whose mother happens to be Indigenous) reveals how ILAs are
intimately bound up with whites' desire to appropriate the Indigenous
persona as well.

WHITE FATHER (THE WANNABE INDIAN): I'll say this,
though. These transplants sure can make some ice cream.
SON: What's a transplant?
WHITE FATHER: It's, um . . . a person who moves to a place,
and then they try to make that place just like the place
they left.
SON: That don't make sense.
WHITE FATHER: No, not one bit.

The *Yellowstone* transplants are, of course, recent settlers gentrifying older settler towns. However, unlike the initial white homesteaders or pioneers who first "gentrified" Indigenous Peoples' living spaces, *Yellowstone* casts the descendants of the initial homesteaders or pioneers in the "role of Indians." Like the Indians of yesteryear, they fight against modern development in order to maintain their way of life, ranching—that is, the freedom to do anything you want on "their land." But the narrative is flipped in such a way that even "casino Indians" are threatening the self-indigenizing settler. Sound familiar? It should.

Perhaps inundated with messaging that confuses their "right" to occupy Indigenous lands illegally, settlers feel that invoking an ILA is the best they can do. ILAs may poorly mimic customary Indigenous Land Acknowledgments, but an ontological distinctness haunts these ILAs. A foundational rift lies between settlers' land acknowledgments and how Indigenous Peoples acknowledge land, such as sacred places. Despite enlightened settler protest to the contrary, for the former, land is foremost a resource in service of Western development; that is, infrastructure, profit making, and a defined civilization (for example, private property). For the latter, land is not so. For example, compare the following Indigenous Land Acknowledgment, which I wrote and use following my email signature, to performative ILAs:

> Greetings from my homeland, the Očhéthi Šakówiŋ
> Oyáte Makȟóčhe. Our homeland is where our relatives
> come from, where our relatives live, and where our rela-
> tives love and defend each other. To co-exist with our
> relatives is a difficult responsibility but one made more so
> ever since settlers invaded our homeland. Settlers, among
> other things, have nearly exterminated our relative, the
> Tȟatȟaŋka Oyáte. Compared to 150 years ago, few of
> them survive today. Settlers have enclosed our relative,
> the Mni Oyáte. There are several structures built on the
> Mníšóše that, like bondage, constrain their natural, life-
> giving flow. Settlers have drilled into our relative, Uŋčí
> Makȟá. The drilling has left our Grandmother Earth with
> notable scars: Mount Rushmore, Crazy Horse Monument,
> Homestake Mine, Dakota Access Pipeline, and abandoned
> radiation testing sites. Settlers have illegally colonized
> and, therefore, unlawfully reside in our homeland. We
> have never consented to these and other colonizer-led
> harms. Hence, the litmus test of any land acknowledgment
> is the rightful return of stolen Native land.

What distinguishes my ILA from the current spate of settler ILAs is its language and message. My ILA speaks of an Indigenous person who is centered at the receiving end of settler colonialism's violence and abuse. An unsanitized ILA, then, explicitly names the land's original inhabitants, names the harms (as a result of wrongdoing), identifies the perpetrators and who they harmed, and proposes, among other things, a reparative justice action/restorative justice response. Indeed, though almost all ILA statements fail to mention returning stolen Indigenous land or any other reparative justice action, at the very least they may trigger a starting point for protecting sacred places.

Since ILAs do not preclude settlers from talking with Indigenous Peoples about protecting places they know to be sacred, some clarifications can further the dialogue of how reparative justice might, in conjunction with ILAs, be used to protect sacred places. First, many people understandably associate reparative justice with reparations. While reparative justice and reparations may overlap and share common elements, they serve different purposes. In the Western world, for instance, reparation is grounded in the Western legal tradition, particularly for criminal justice. From this context, nomenclature and processes frame reparation as an individualized matter—the "offender" and the "victim." Moreover, since criminal justice systems are arms of the state, they take control of the harm that individuals inflict on others. For a victim, then, justice is ostensibly served when the state finds an offender guilty. Beyond custodial punishment, the state may also require the offender to pay a fine (punitive and/or compensatory damages) as a form of reparation to the victim.

Second, the international community recognizes that, in addition to individuals, state and/or corporate actors can harm individuals who share a common attribute or attributes. For example, here in the United States, while enslaving millions of individuals of Indigenous African descent until December 1865 and "granting" them US citizenship in July 1868, the nation nonetheless condoned a very violent and lethal regime of forced racial segregation against them until the civil rights movement. Moreover, before the civil war among white US settlers over slavery, settlers forcibly removed (that is, ethnically cleansed) hundreds of thousands of Indigenous Peoples east of the Mississippi River. During World War II, settlers interned about 120,000 individual US citizens who happened to be of Japanese ancestry.

By definition, reparation means a national government takes political action to right a historic wrong and its enduring effects. In other words, reparation is about making amends and putting things right. The wrongs involve a national government's human-rights violations that have, on its citizenry's behalf, been perpetrated against a targeted population. Reparations and righting wrongs are, in practice, very specific. Through the United Nations, the international community, building on a variety of conventions, has operationalized this definition in the following manner:[19]

- **Restitution** restores the situation that existed before the wrongful act(s) were committed, such as restoring liberty or employment, returning to the places of residence, and returning property;
- **Compensation** provides monetary payment for "economically assessable damage" arising from the violation, including physical harm, mental harm, material losses, and lost opportunities;
- **Rehabilitation** provides "medical and psychological care as well as legal and social services" to aid individual and collective recovery;
- **Satisfaction** includes a range of measures that restore the presence of justice. These measures may involve truth-telling, statements aimed at ending ongoing abuses, commemorations or tributes to the victims, preserving historical memory, witnessing expressions of regret or formal apologies for wrongdoing; and
- **Guarantees of non-repetition** include institutional and legal reforms as well as reforms to government practices to end the abuse.

Japanese Americans, for example, received monetary reparations for their unlawful internment during World War II.[20] African Americans, since the end of the whites' civil war in 1865, have called for reparations for the mass harms of slavery and its ongoing legacy of harm. In February 2021, Dreisen Heath, an expert on Black reparations and reparatory justice, submitted written testimony on H.R. 40, a bill to establish the Commission to Study and Develop Reparation Proposals for African Americans. An excerpt from her testimony shows that US reparations to the Black community would likely include all five elements.

> The failure to account for the historic racial and gendered injustices of slavery and its legacy has compounded the harm and fueled the persistence of racial inequality today. Enduring racist and classist structures remain in place and accumulated racial discrimination has gone unaddressed. . . . A holistic inquiry into these injustices and the ways subsequent policy has created and reinforced structures and systems that have prevented Black people from advancing is urgently needed, as is a plan to provide reparation and healing for these harms.[21]

Before any meaningful reparation, however, a targeted population must find allies who can help engage others in an educational campaign, move society's conscience to act on its moral values, and persistently lobby its national government for redress. Targeted populations (such as Japanese Americans and Black communities) discover, though, that despite overwhelming and damming evidence, it still takes several generations for reparations actually to materialize. If they do materialize, a national government and its citizenry may feel a debt has been settled, and it is time to move on. Finally, these examples would indicate that settler-inflicted harms have been and continue to be premised on race, a common, if not primary, distinction—except when settler harms are perpetrated against Indigenous Peoples.

My use of Indigenous *Peoples* rather than people, population, group, minority, or tribe/tribal is intentional.[22] ILAs and reparative justice must keep this distinction foremost when a collaborative, Indigenous-led action is taken to protect sacred places. Julian Burger, a white settler who worked with the UN Working Group on Indigenous populations (UNWGIP), noted how the term *peoples*, when appendaged to Indigenous, becomes politically volatile: it invariably triggers fragility among settler people, institutions, and states:

> Along with these international institutions [e.g., ILO, HRC], national governments [e.g., Canada, Australia, New Zealand, and United States] tend to view their indigenous peoples as national minorities or minority populations requiring special treatment or consideration. They are a population recognized as different from the majority or dominant group, but implicitly a part of the total national identity. *International organizations and national governments both carefully avoid referring to indigenous minorities as peoples because such a term carries with it the notion of self-determination.*[23]

This "notion" of self-determination that Burger alluded to is, in fact, international law. The United Nations recognizes that peoples—not national minorities or minority populations—have a *right* to self-determination. Indeed, Indigenous communities and settler states had a heated debate over adding an "s" to "people." As an excerpt from a March 2022 joint declaration of an Indigenous alliance shows, settlers employ terminology that willfully fails to recognize Indigenous Peoples' nationhood.

> We, Original Nations and Indigenous Peoples of Mother Earth, also consider the use of the word "populations" in operative paragraph 4 of the United Nations Human Rights Council Resolution 48/7, to diminish our status as nations and peoples, create ambiguity, and violate our rights of self-determination as nations and peoples.[24]

Unlike Indigenous Peoples, whose sovereignties predate the establishment of the United States and Canada, national minorities or minority populations have neither a nation-to-nation nor a treaty relationship with the countries of their citizenship. And because treaties are internationally recognized instruments that countries routinely use when dealing with one another, whatever "special treatment or consideration" we receive or obtain from the US settler state is primarily because of our political status, not our racial status. Any action proposing to protect sacred places, then, must keep front and center our right of self-determination and our nation-to-nation relationship; both settlers and our peoples need to remember this political relationship and recognize our sovereignty as the basis for action. Because of these two points, reparative justice lends itself to protecting sacred places.

Fortunately, folks in the Mennonite community provide a working definition of reparative justice for Indigenous Peoples and settlers to consider when implementing our goal to protect sacred places.

> Reparative justice refers to a spectrum of actions on the part of settlers and Christians that seek—to the fullest extent possible—to repair harms done to Indigenous Peoples as a result of the Doctrine of [Christian] Discovery, to put an end to ongoing harm, and to restore Indigenous sovereignty and lands. These actions should be responsive to the context and needs of Indigenous groups, and may include solidarity actions, land return, financial restitution, and advocacy for just laws and policies.[25]

This reparative framework is adaptable to a wide range of settler–Indigenous circumstances. After all, settler-led land development has harmed (and continues to harm), disrupted (and continues to disrupt), and altered (and continues to alter) the places we love and know to be sacred. Discussions aimed at protecting sacred lands should therefore center around harm: naming who is being or has been harmed and who is doing harm; repairing past harm(s); stopping present harm(s); and not repeating the harm(s) through proactive prevention. Compensatory restitution (paying for harm through "land claim" settlements) becomes less of a factor when we focus on how we envision protection. Since we have ample evidence of how settlers, both as individuals and through their governments, have harmed Indigenous Peoples, we do not need to rehash already known harms—ILAs and Indigenous-led actions against development that threaten cultural areas name these in spades. Protecting sacred places is the starting point. Addressing, undoing, and repairing settler-based harms to sacred places necessarily involves acknowledging the ceremonies that go with these places.

While the settlers' theft of our homelands will always remain the First Harm, protecting sacred places is a more immediate concern stemming from settlers' theft. Most often, Western development desecrates and harms sacred places. For example, the San Carlos Apache and others fight to protect Chi'Chil Bildagoteel (also known as Oak Flats). Since time immemorial, Apache people have known Chi'Chil Bildagoteel to be a sacred area where they hold cultural ceremonies. The fight involves opposing a land swap that would include Chi'Chil Bildagoteel between copper mining interests and the US settler state. In the north, the Anishinaabeg people fight to protect wild rice and other cultural practices from Enbridge's Line 3 pipeline project, which trespasses on treaty-secured areas. Finally, the Wet'suwet'en people fight against Coastal GasLink's pipeline. This pipeline would transport fracked gas through Wet'suwet'en unceded territory, and its construction is having—and will continue to have—an adverse impact on the Wet'suwet'en and their homeland. They are modeling a higher principle—protecting sacred places—that many settler institutions, such as the Army Corps of Engineers or the Royal Bank of Canada and other settler institutions, fail to protect. For Indigenous Peoples, protecting sacred places trumps ethical, aesthetic, conservation, or development considerations. These North American examples demonstrate an ontological gap between us and settlers—a profound difference in how we Indigenous Peoples understand reality and what it means to exist here. To be sure, Indigenous sacred lands defenders and their allies deserve our gratitude.

Vine Deloria Jr. often spoke about sacred places; he proposed at least four kinds of sacred lands.[26] One type is human contrived. When something of great importance transpires at a place, people display reverence at the site. For my nation, the 1876 Pȟežísla Wakpá Okíčhize, the 1890 Oyáte Owíčhakte at Wounded Knee, or the sites where 1851 and 1868 Fort Laramie Treaties took place fall in this group. The remaining sacred places are Higher-Power stamped. In other words, Higher Powers intervene in human activities to

- mark a place of spiritual significance (for example, Mathó-Pahá, Mathó Thípila);
- "reveal Themselves to human beings," which makes such places overwhelmingly sacred (for example, Ȟesápa Ki); or
- become "actively involved in human activities to chart out a new historical course for humans" (for example, Pte Sáŋ Wiŋ, Wičháȟpi Hiŋȟpáya).[27]

The last type is the most critical. New revelations at different places likely mean new ceremonies. To Indigenous eyes, these experiences of the sacred prove that the Higher Powers are neither dead nor mere bystanders but are active in human affairs. In response, Indigenous spiritual or cultural practitioners or knowledge keepers know that adhering to certain ceremonies at certain places at certain times of the year defines our moral responsibility. Otherwise, the Higher Powers, the Natural World, and the nonhuman peoples who inhabit the Natural World might wonder what happened to us—and we might ask that question among ourselves, too.

Absent this moral imperative, Deloria observed that the sacred becomes secularized, and because of that transition (from the sacred to the secular), we experience harms:

> Sacred places are the foundation of all other beliefs and practices because they represent the presence of the sacred in our lives. They properly inform us that we are not larger than nature and that we have responsibilities to the rest of the natural world that transcend our own personal desires and wishes. This lesson must be learned by each generation; unfortunately, the technology of industrial society always leads us in the other direction. Yet it is certain that as we permanently foul our planetary nest, we shall have to learn a bitter lesson. There is probably not sufficient time for the non-Indian population to understand the meaning of sacred lands and incorporate the idea into their lives and practices. We can but hope that some protection can be afforded [to] these sacred places before the world becomes wholly secular and is destroyed.[28]

Deloria called it right: perhaps a paradigm shift is now moot because it is already too late. Climate changes worldwide reveal that we are indeed learning a hard lesson about fouling our nest—Indigenous Peoples are prophetic. How many "Indian Wisdom" books have been published about the folly of Western thought and philosophy? How long have settlers read these books yet rejected the changes they call for? Westernization marches on, trampling over sacred places and their preservation and use. I am reminded of one of our songs, "He Sapa Ki, Un Kita Pi."[29] The song speaks to our collective responsibility to the Black Hills—a responsibility given to us by our Higher Powers. Knowing how settlers' activities and development desecrate the Black Hills, which includes climate change's vagaries, my people find this song deeply moving. It says that, despite the Black Hills' desecration, we cannot abandon our responsibilities. We still do—and must do—specific ceremonies at specific places at specific times of the year, otherwise the Natural World could rightly ask us, "What has become of you?" "Why do you neglect your responsibilities to us? "Are we not your relative?" To risk such a reckoning, no matter the circumstance, is not an option for us: abandoning our responsibilities is, for us, unfathomable.

IS AMERICA IRREDEEMABLE?

Almost four decades have passed since Sutton wrote his settler-reassuring prolegomenon in *Irredeemable America*. Embedded in Sutton's prolegomenon is both settler colonialism and white settler fragility. Settler colonialism instills settlers with the primary motivation to eliminate Indigenous Peoples. Eliminating us allows settlers to access our territories and establish their inauthentic national identity (as Americans, Canadians, and so on). Perhaps Sutton and others engage in settler bravado, a form of self-deception substituting for reality. After all, Sutton told us unequivocally that America is irredeemable, right? His prolegomenon affirms that the Christians' Doctrine of Discovery is the starting point and the final authority for settlers "having" absolute title to Indigenous lands—our lands.

White and other settlers often respond with settler fragility, portraying themselves as innocent victims whenever we question their legitimacy in our traditional territories. For example, John Christie Jr., a white settler and lawyer who defended other property-owning settlers against an Indigenous nation's 1978 land claim, provided the following rationale for his clients' innocence:

> If there was a historical injustice done to the Indians, the
> United States was generally the culprit—either because
> it assisted in the taking of the land or failed to prevent the
> taking, contrary to its constitutional obligations to act as
> guardian of Indian tribal interest. . . . As one historian has
> observed: "By standing on the sidelines as Indians and non-
> Indians fight these bitter court battles, the federal govern-
> ment has encouraged an impression that Indian advances
> can be made only at the expense of non-Indians who did
> not commit the acts alleged as the basis of the suit." *Surely
> there is a basic inequity as well in forcing present-day landowners
> to defend themselves against ancient claims that are in no sense based
> upon any wrongdoing on their part.* . . . To the extent that there
> may be any legal or moral basis to the Indian claims, they
> deserve to be addressed or remedied by the federal gov-
> ernment, which ought to bear the burden of having failed
> to act over the years.[30]

For settlers to blame their government for their predicament when Indigenous Peoples press for land restoration, as in protecting sacred places, is disingenuous in the extreme. With very rare exceptions, settlers did not scream foul when their government initially stole (and continues to steal) our land on their behalf. In fact, they continue to benefit from such theft.

However, like so many other settlers before and after him, Sutton acknowledged but grossly misjudged the power that reparative justice carries. Its moral force continues even in the face of overwhelming wrongdoing, past or present. Yet, despite the harms below, Sutton boldly concludes that irredeemability is a self-evident truth—that the majority of white settlers are unwilling to "give back" land to Indigenous Peoples:

- Settlers perpetrate wrongful deeds without the expectation of ever being held accountable, even though accountability is necessary for justice.
- Indigenous Peoples are aggrieved over our lands being wrongfully taken when our call for land return means genuine reconciliation.
- Indigenous Peoples are aggrieved over having only one recourse for justice—the litigation process—that settlers would allow or consider.
- Even though settlers declare constitutionally that treaties are "the supreme Law of the Land," our expectations for an honorable resolution for the wrongful taking of our lands have not been met.

Irredeemability, then, displays classic settler hubris and fragility, and of course, defends the indefensible. Hence, settlers embrace an illusion of assured irredeemability when it comes to Indigenous lands. This illusion is what guides settlers' structures of feeling and steers their attitudes and emotions into rationalizing their theft and illegal occupation of our homelands. Settler expectations, formalized in legal, institutional, and cultural processes, lock settlers into believing they are entitled to our homelands. These expectations drive fantasies of settler entitlement (internalized privilege), all without any basis in reality. Therefore, settlers' out-of-hand dismissals of what is possible will not stand. Think about it: How can settlers "give land back" when it was never theirs to give? The only recourse left is for them to return the lands they stole.

Yet, settlers' out-of-hand dismissals of what is possible will not fly. This special issue of the *Wicazo Sa Review* shows that unresolved harms around Indigenous land claims, including protecting sacred lands—long thought irredeemable—persist in unforeseen ways.

The numerous ILAs, the myriad of US statutes and policies requiring consultation with Indigenous Peoples,[31] numerous Native laws and policies regarding cultural patrimony (such as Standing Rock Sioux Tribe's Title 32 Cultural Resource Code), and various international conventions, such the original UNDRIP,[32] convey to settlers that we Indigenous Peoples have bought neither their assumptions nor their fantasies.

We have our starting points too (like our respective origin stories), our final authorities (like our sacred places, our significant landmarks), and our cultural areas (like our national homelands, treaty recognized or not), all of which predate settler presence in North America. Protecting sacred places, then, involves more than settlers realize or are willing to admit. According to Sutton, the settlers' intention not to restore and return stolen Indigenous lands—or even to protect sacred places—is what makes America irredeemable. To be sure, that is one take on irredeemability, but it is not the last word.

Another aspect of irredeemability concerns the moral universe, one that we all live in but which settlers do not consider when protecting sacred places. Space limitations prevent me from taking a deep dive into an Indigenous perspective about the absence of the sacred among settlers. I leave readers to ponder the implications. Whereas ILAs, reparative justice, and sacred places situate themselves within this moral universe, Americans' irredeemability assumes a far different and deeply worrisome moral dilemma. Substantive reparative justice and critical ILAs are not tokens or merely symbolic gestures; neither are Indigenous commitments to protecting sacred places and ensuring access to them.

Settlers in the United States are taught to perceive themselves as good people whose morality is beyond reproach. However, the irredeemability of the moral kind we discuss in this special journal issue makes settlers confront a grim reality: They may have long since forfeited the moral high ground. This forfeiture becomes painfully evident to settlers when their actions stand in contrast to Indigenous Peoples' moral responsibilities. Our moral responsibilities to sacred places underscore to settlers that they do not stand at or near the moral universe's center. Instead, they find themselves along its fringes, looking disquietly inward. Their core beliefs, such as American exceptionalism or the American dream, tell settlers who they are. But when they stand on the very fringes of the moral universe far from its center, settlers find their beliefs about themselves unraveling. Nonetheless, as this special issue of the *Wicazo Sa Review* shows, a redemptive pathway back into this moral universe may yet be possible for them. If so, it begins, at the very minimum, with settlers first protecting—and then returning—our sacred places.

Waŋblí Wapȟáha Hokšíla (Edward Charles Valandra) is Síčáŋǧu Thithuŋwaŋ, born and raised in his homeland, the Očhéthi Šakówiŋ Oyáte Makȟóčhe. He received his BA from Minnesota State University–Mankato, his MA from the University of Colorado–Boulder, and his PhD from SUNY–Buffalo. Dr. Valandra's current role is senior editor at Living Justice Press, a small, nonprofit publisher specializing in peacemaking Circles, restorative justice, and addressing harms between Peoples. He is the editor of *Colorizing Restorative Justice: Voicing Our Realities* and author of *Not Without Our Consent: Lakota Resistance to Termination, 1950–1959*, and is the editor of the forthcoming book, *Colorizing Circle Practices: Naming the Silences*.

1   Roy Brooks recognizes the substantive difference between reparation and settlement:

> Responses that seek atonement for the commission of an injustice are properly called *reparations*. Responses in which the government does not express atonement are more suitably called *settlements*. The latter can be analogized to their use in American law. Often a defendant corporation [US government in Indigenous land claim cases] will settle a dispute by signing a consent decree in which it agrees to pay the plaintiff(s) a certain sum of money, but does not concede any wrongdoing. In fact, both parties stipulate that the defendant has *not* violated any law. A settlement is less a victory than a compromise. It gives the victim a monetary award (not necessarily enough to cover actual losses) and gives the perpetrator a chance to end the dispute without a finding of liability. Usually, a reparation is easily distinguish-able from a settlement by the presence or absence of an accompanying statement of apology. Roy L. Brooks, "The Age of Apology," in *When Sorry Isn't Enough*, ed. Roy L. Brooks (New York: New York University Press, 1999), 8–9.

See also Edward Charles Valandra's "The *Cobell v. Salazar* Settlement Offers Inadequate Compensation and Lacks Important Provisions," in *Native Americans: Opposing Viewpoints Series*, ed. Lynn M. Zott (Farmington Hills, MI: GreenHaven Press, 2012).

2   *Prolegomenon* is defined as "a formal essay or critical discussion serving to introduce and interpret an extended work" (*Merriam-Webster Online Dictionary*). Like in theological studies, in *Irredeemable America* Sutton uses his prolegomenon to set up how readers view and understand Indigenous peoples' land tenure. Being a settler, Sutton makes certain that his and other settlers' viewpoints are accepted as doctrinaire. Most importantly for him, his prolegomenon lays out the notion that land return or restoration is, for Indigenous peoples, nothing more than a pipe dream. For more about prolegomena, see "What Is a Prolegomena?" Got Questions Ministries, https://www.got questions.org/prolegomena.html.

3   Imre Sutton, "Prolegomena," in *Irredeemable America, The Indians' Estate and Land Claims*, ed. Imre Sutton (Albuquerque: University of New Mexico Press, 1985), 4. Emphasis mine.

4   Sutton, "Prolegomena," 5–6. Emphasis mine.

5   Andrew Woolford and Amanda Nelund, *The Politics of Restorative Justice: A Critical Introduction*, 2nd ed. (Halifax and Winnipeg: Fernwood, 2019), 191.

6   See *Irredeemable America*, 113–14, for a brief summary of aboriginal title versus recognized title.

7   Michael Asch, "Post-Calder, Canada's Judiciary Struggles to Reconfigure Native Rights," *Cultural Survival Quarterly Magazine*, March 2004, https://www.culturalsurvival.org/publications/cultural-survival-quarterly/post-calder-canadas-judiciary-struggles-reconfigure-native.

8   Asch, "Post-Calder." Emphasis mine.

9   See Thomas E. Keefe, "Land Acknowledgment: A Trend in Higher Education and Nonprofit Organizations," *Research Gate*, https://doi.org/10.13140/RG.2.2.33681.07521.

10   Stephen Marche, "Canada's Impossible Acknowledgment," *The New Yorker*, September 7, 2017, https://www.newyorker.com/culture/culture-desk/canadas-impossible-acknowledgment.

11   SCMS 2018 Conference Program, Toronto, Ontario, March 14–18, 2018, 1, https://cdn.ymaws.com/www.cmstudies.org/resource/resmgr/2018_conference/scms2018iprogram-no_rooms.pdf. The SCMS conference booklet included a land acknowledgement statement as well.

12   Marche, "Canada's Impossible Acknowledgment."

13   Marche, "Canada's Impossible Acknowledgment."

14   "Land Acknowledgment," SCMS 2018 Conference Program.

15   Elisa J. Sobo, Michael Lambert, and Valerie Lambert, "Land Acknowledgments Meant to Honor Indigenous People Too Often Do the Opposite—Erasing American Indians and Sanitizing History Instead," *The Conversation*, November 8, 2021, https://theconversation.com/land-acknowledgments-meant-to-honor-indigenous-people-too-often-do-the-opposite-erasing-american-indians-and-sanitizing-history-instead-163787.

16   1868 Fort Laramie Treaty, Article 2. The US settler state also recognizes our national boundaries in this article and in Article 16. Emphasis mine.

17   Marche, "Canada's Impossible Acknowledgment."

18   Sobo et al., "Land Acknowledgments."

19   See United Nations, "Basic Principles and Guidelines on the Rights to a Remedy and Reparations for Victims of Gross Violations of International Human Rights Law and Serious Violations of International Humanitarian Law," UN General Assembly Resolution 60/147, December 16, 2005.

20   The Civil Liberties Act of 1988 (P.L. 100-383) is a US settler reparations law for the unlawful detention and internment during World War II of US citizens of Japanese ancestry.

21   Dreisen Heath, "H.R. 40: Exploring the Path to Reparative Justice in America," written

testimony to the US House Committee on the Judiciary, Subcommittee on the Constitution, Civil Rights, and Civil Liberties, February 17, 2021, p. 4, https://www.hrw.org/news /2021/02/17/hr-40-exploring -path-reparative-justice-america#.

22 "American Indian" is a racial, not political, status. In a settler-racialized society or state, the use of "American Indian" or "Native American" collapses thousands of Indigenous peoples, who are citizens of their respective sovereign Native Nations, into one homogenous racial group. As a result, most settlers, and to some degree Indigenous people, see treaty rights, privileges, and immunities as race-based rather than as inherent in our political status. The use of "tribe" or "tribal" represents Indigenous Peoples as possessing a highly compromised sovereignty. For example, settlers define *tribal sovereignty* as meaning "domestic dependent nation." Therefore, Indigenous Peoples can, with severe settler-imposed restrictions, exercise "self-government" but not self-determination.

23 Julian Berger, *Report from the Frontier: The State of the World's Indigenous Peoples* (London: Zed Books, 1978), 8. Emphasis mine.

24 See 1894 Great Sioux Nation Treaty Council, "A Joint Declaration from the Following Indigenous Nations and Peoples to the United Nations Secretary General, High Commissioner for Human Rights, Human Rights Council, Committee on the Elimination of Racial Discrimination, and the Expert Mechanism on the Rights of Indigenous Peoples," March 18, 2022. This declaration outlines six points pertaining to (1) support for Human Rights Council Resolution 48/7, "Negative impact of the legacies of colonialism on the enjoyment of human rights, which would apply to Indigenous Peoples in North, Central, South America"; (2) participation in the UN decolonization process; (3) support for Special Rapporteur Miguel Alfonso Martínez's 1999 UN Study on Treaties, Agreements, and Constructive Arrangements; (4) opposing the Expert Mechanism on the Rights of Indigenous Peoples' study of "Treaties, agreements, and other constructive arrangements, between indigenous peoples and States, including peace accords and reconciliation initiatives, and their constitutional recognition"; (5) clarifying the negative impact of the term "populations" in Resolution 48/7; and (6) asserting the "right to address all forms and manifestations of colonialism, foreign occupation . . . and genocide on an equal basis to all other peoples and nations in accordance with the United Nations Charter." Author's file.

25 Katerina Friesen, introduction to *Stories of Repair: A Reparative Justice Resource Toward Dismantling the Doctrine of Discovery*, ed. Katherina Friesen (Phoenix AZ: Dismantling the Doctrine of Discovery Coalition, 2021), 8.

26 Indeed, Vine Deloria Jr. was very clear about approaching the topic of sacred lands. He said, "If we were to subject the topic of the sacredness of land to a western rational analysis, fully recognizing that such an analysis is merely for our convenience in discussion and does not represent the nature of reality." *God Is Red: A Native View of Religion*, 2nd ed. (Golden CO: Fulcrum, 1994), 271.

27 Deloria, *God Is Red*, 272–77.

28 Deloria, *God Is Red*, 281–82.

29 Earl Bullhead, *Keeper of the Drum*, Sound of America Records, 1995.

The Lakota lyrics of this song
are "Tȟuŋkašila ȟe sápa ki
tȟawamakȟiya ca / Lehaŋ e otéȟi
wákhiyaheya he . . . he welo."
Bullhead's free translation:
"Grandfather, you have given us
the responsibility of the Black
Hills. Up to this day, I'm doing
the best that I can."

30 John C. Christie Jr., "Indian Land
Claims Involving Private Owners
of Land," in Sutton, *Irredeemable
America*, 242. Emphasis mine.

31 1906 Antiquities Act; 1936
Historic Sites Act; 1966 National
Historic Preservation Act
as amended; 1970 National
Environmental Policy Act; 1974
Archaeological and Historic
Preservation Act; 1978 America
Indian and Religious Freedom
Act; 1979 Archeological
Resources Protection Act;
1990 Native America Graves
Protection and Repatriation
Act; 1996 Executive Order
13007, Indian Sacred Sites; and
2000 Executive Order 13175,
Consultation and Coordination
with Indian Tribal Governments.

32 See Charmaine White Face's
*Indigenous Rights in the Balance: An
Analysis of the Declaration on the
Rights of Indigenous Peoples* (St. Paul:
Living Justice Press, 2013) for the
original draft of the UNDRIP.

"My Old People Used to Say . . ."
Reflections on Sacred Places in Tuwaduq Territories of the Pacific Northwest

Hon. Sm3tcoom Delbert Miller, as told to and edited with Tina Kuckkahn

This article is written in interview format, to preserve the tradition of oral history as practiced by numerous Indigenous cultures. Interviewer Tina Kuckkahn (Lac du Flambeau Ojibwe) engages Skokomish spiritual leader Sm3tcoom Delbert Miller to explore concepts of what makes certain places in the Hood Canal region of the Pacific Northwest's Olympic Peninsula sacred. Culturally trained since the age of four, Sm3tcoom shares his perspective as an elder who carries on the traditions and relays the teachings of his ancestors to the next generations.

TINA KUCKKAHN: When asked to talk about how the teachings you share today are influenced by your ancestors, you often begin with: "My old people used to say. . . ." Can you talk about what that means to you?

HON. SM3TCOOM DELBERT MILLER: What it means to me when I say "my old people used to say" is that I'm listening to them right now, and I can begin to hear them converse. It's as if I'm with them right now. That's what they used to say, is that they may be gone, but we still have conversations. This is a very important part of the training and the teachings of our culture and how important it is to be spiritually connected, in a manner of speaking.

What makes this so beautiful? The training of these areas of teachings, we would call *stu wha schu lu*.[1] It means the ancestral law in the Twana language. We are to remember our ancestral law, the village places, the family trees, and the ceremonies. We are to remember the life of the people at all of the villages, who did things that were noted, what happened at these villages, these numerous sacred places.

Some of them are very sacred from what we would call our Changer, our Creator, in a manner of speaking, or it could be something about where a village had once been. It could be places where somebody received a sacred power, a spirit. One specific thing I want to refer to or talk about in this is they used to say that you begin to teach your children to have a place that you love. They would begin to take you to places then and begin to encourage you and praise you and say very beautiful and loving things, give you beautiful teachings in various places.

It was a very significant thing to do, because what they were really doing was taking the young people to find a place they loved. And it was oftentimes an old village place or a place where a ceremony that a person had done, maybe several generations ago, maybe a little longer, maybe even more recent. The ceremony that our old people did was they would go to a place they loved and they would leave things there. If they were a carver, in that place they loved, they would leave their carving implements. A weaver would leave their weaving tools. A fisherman might leave some things related to the kind of fisherman they were. Those were left at a place they loved. The reason was very important. It would be so that later on, generations later, from time to time, when they got lonesome for that place that they loved, even if they'd been gone maybe several hundred years, they would get to return to that place they loved and visit and dwell there for a period of time.

That's what made some of these places very significant to our families was that they would begin to take the young people to those types of places and teach them things there, tell them very important things, and begin to raise or stand their life up to be very important and significant. As they did it, there began to be a place that these young people loved. It would oftentimes be a direct lineal grandchild of the people who were there and who left things they loved in this particular place. The grandchild would love that place now, and they would begin to return on their own, with the hopes and the prayers for doing such a training for their young people. This place now became sacred to the family lineage and the family's inherited rights would pass through at that place.

That place would be referred to as *patiya a uqwalth*, meaning the grandparents of grandparents of grandparents of grandparents of grandparents. Who knows—maybe all the way back to the beginning of time. Those grandparents oftentimes went back to that place they loved. Now, this grandchild of all these people would return to that place they loved. The prayer was that maybe they would have an encounter with an ancestor, because all of those grandparents took the time to leave something at that one particular place. So the grandchildren now would be trained at many of these kinds of places in hopes that they would find a spirit, something that would be inherited from these ancestors. *Patiya a uckwalth* means all those lineal grandparents. *At ti shlu al bud* means the inherited gifts that come down that lineage. So that's why it was so very significant to remember the old village places and who lived there.

What kinds of things happened there? What spirits did they receive there? What ceremonies did they do there? What was so significant in the family lineages? That's what they would be handing down to all of the young people. Some of the young people got so very knowledgeable about all these places that the old people would return to, that they began to be leaders in training, leaders in certain spiritual developments. Maybe the people wanted to have a fisherman or hunter or carver or weaver, and maybe this person who had been highly trained, now would take those young people and show them how to seek, how to go to the place they loved, how to utter the names of all the people that dwelled and roamed and lived in these places and tell them all the sacred things that had taken place.

Now, that's the formation of a sacred place. The old people used to say to remember the place you love and always return there. If it was near water, they would train the young people. If they had been away from it for a certain amount of time, they would have to wade into that water just to their ankles when it was cold, until it began to tingle. Now that young person would once again be tied back to that sacred connection place with the old people, they would be grounded now in life. If it was on land, they would wait until it snowed, and they would stand up to their ankles in the snow and walk in until they began to tingle in their feet from being cold. Now they're being grounded in life again to that land where the old people once roamed and lived, in hopes that there would be a spiritual connection one day, because we're grounded back to the land, a place our old people loved, and our young people loved.

It would also give them something to look forward to, which was something very sacred. That's one type of way to connect to the land. They used to tell the people the ways that are so sacred, that they have to learn to listen to the river, how to listen to life, how to listen to the land, the brush. When the hunters would be trained, they would be taught how to spiritually see and hear and feel and sense. They would be communicated to when game was in the area. The grass would be telling them that game was there. They would take a baby to the mountains and do a ceremony for their feet and introduce them to that place for their future training and seeking place. It was taught that the baby would never go without in life because they would get help from the others that left something in that place they loved.

Also, the people who were seeking healing or a healing spirit, they had to be connected by listening to the land, the wind, depending on the kind of spirit they were seeking, and again at a place that they were seeking was at the land they loved, and that our old people would be there.

They had to be trained to get down to the very bottom of their soul. From there, they would begin to listen. All of their soul would be trained to listen to the sacred thoughts, to see all of the sacredness, to hear and to feel sacredness. Once they began to learn and understand how to listen in that manner, to hear the goodness of life, see the goodness of life, breathe the sacredness of life, they now began to be connected to all of the land. There were trainers who would take the young people and train them on how to be connected to everything in their spiritual seeking.

Their main job was to train young people how to seek the connection to our old people to teach them all of the sacred places, the village places. They were highly honored, those people that knew how to train. They would take the young people to these places and begin to teach them how to listen to the goodness of life, how to listen from the bottom of their soul, how to listen to the river, how to listen to life, how to listen to everything they feel.

As they got deeper into their training, they would tell the young people, "Now you have to swim," and they would tell them: "Take your hat off and go put it on that bush. Take your shirt off and put it on that little rock over there. Take your shoes and put them by that clump of grass."

They would now tell them to sit there and listen, because all of these things in their surroundings were being dressed. Now they would begin to speak and they became a part of that training there. If young people were being taught how to be a speaker, they would begin to speak to all of these things that they dressed. Those were training places, and they would have special markings, maybe a petroglyph, maybe a certain plank, or something that was carved and left there at these places.

Now, if they were to have a fisherman for training, they would take them to particular places where they may inherit a gift to fish. The trainer would carve a pole that they would drive in right at the edge of the water. The particular kind of power they wanted that young person to train with and seek and receive would be carved into this pole. If they received a spirit with it, then that's where they built their fish traps and their fishing places. They would use their power to call the fish back to that spot, because those were representative of the power they received through the training in a place they loved. Now, our old people used to say, to be able to understand the kind of spirit you have, if it was a fisherman, they taught them what to do with the salmon or the kind of fish they received—how to feed them there and how to leave food for them, and how to take care of that particular fish.

For hunters, they took them oftentimes to a place where their old people loved to hunt and had their summer villages. They would train them on how to seek in those places, in the place they loved, and that the hunters would leave a particular spear or a knife or a bow in certain places. Over the centuries, this would have occurred many times. Now, as a boy, my dad showed me a place, and in this place he was showing me, we were walking among the trees. Suddenly, he looked up into a tree and there was a very old gaff hook hanging up in a very old tree. He didn't know how long that must have been there, but it had been there a very long time. He wouldn't allow us to go get it. He had us leave it there, but yet we had to go there from time to time and pray and be in that place, because that had been left there by somebody; that meant it was somebody's place that they loved and where they received a power for fishing.

Our old people used to say we begin to pray and learn how to seek as a child. There will be a place that we would be drawn to. We begin to ask to go there. Sometimes it began to be that those old people, our old people, would come to speak and sing to us. Our old people would say, "Oh, you better go over to that place right over on that beach, because that's where old so-and-so lived, who had that kind of song." We would go there with hopes that we would meet our old people that way. They used to say that there were places where our Creator or Changer, who we call *dukwibahL*, roamed this land.

In one particular sacred place, where the Changer came and was creating the land as it is now, bringing structure, making the colors, and everything was being brought to life. The breath of life was being blown into everything. Well, after quite a while of performing his duties on this earth, he came to a large boulder, his couch, right there at the edge of the heel of Hood Canal. It was a sacred place. This boulder was where *dukwibahL* sat and would take a rest now and took a nap. When he took this nap, he was so sacred that the form of his body was molded into this big, giant rock. It was so sacred that the ground would vibrate and hum, because now *dukwibahL* was there and rested. The rock and the land would vibrate, causing the saltwater of the shore that was right there to glimmer like millions and millions of diamonds on the water.

That was a very sacred place. Well, when the Highway Department was coming through, they were steamrolling everything in their path to make a highway. My grandmother said that they were going to build this highway, and they were going to dynamite that big rock where *dukwibahL* rested, and the people tried to stop the Highway

Department from destroying such a sacred place. But they threatened putting everybody in jail and taking their food away. They had threatened to take their children away. My grandmother said the people were finally pushed back and they began to dynamite that sacred place at the rock. The people, all of the Skokomish people in the surrounding area, were crying and grieving and wailing from such a terrible thing. But the Highway Department destroyed that rock, so they could put a highway through there, when they could have just gone around it. But they decided that's how they'd treat the Skokomish people by going right through their most sacred of places.

Some still go there with the understanding that it's a sacred place where *dukwibahL* rested. They call it *dukwibakL's* couch, where he stopped and rested. Yet only a few families began to tell their children about that place, because the missionaries and the agents said we were not to tell our children about these places, to stop the training. They told the people it was an evil thing to do. Some of the old people used to say, "We will never forget where our old people lived and the sacred places." What makes this sacred is when we did naming ceremonies or dressed the children with the names of these places, the villages. When we name the child, it is called *na'hamet*. It means all that goes with it. In this one sacred place, when they built villages right nearby to where they could feel the ground hum and they would watch the water glisten like millions of diamonds. They would be in awe of seeing and feeling this. The people loved being there.

In such a sacred place, they lived there. One day they began to have naming ceremonies, then they began to have weddings, all of the ceremonies, the healing and the miracles, the teachings, everything. That's the term of *na'hamet*. It means all that goes with it, every stick, every piece of grass, every sparkle from those millions of diamonds on the water, every feeling of the hum of the land, every bit of fog and rain and sun and wind. When the water would breathe, the tide would go in and out, large breaths in and out, in and out, it would be felt more dramatically, more emphatically, more powerfully at that place, because that's where *dukwibahL* was resting and causing the wind, when the tide comes in and out, by breathing there.

The people would go down and feel the wind go back and forth when the tide changed. Breath. When the tide is coming in, the breath would come to the land right at that village. Then it went back out as *dukwibahL* was exhaling, as he was breathing. That was what made this such a sacred place to the people and all of the people that lived there, all of the people that trained there, all of the people that left something that they loved in that land they loved. Our old people used to say, "All of those things go with that name and those inherited rights, teaching and everything that goes with it, goes with that child receiving that name that came from that sacred place, that village site that was nearby."

KUCKKAHN: You've often talked about how places of power were also places of prophecy. Could you share a little about that?

MILLER: In those places were gifts of prophecy and our family lineage. There was a gift of a Pelican power and that Pelican power was a war power, but it also was a prophecy power. In that place, a man had received that Pelican spirit. It gave him the prophecy and he began to tell the people that one day there was going to be a different kind of people coming to this land, and they would turn our world upside down as we once knew it. Meaning, on that day they would begin to talk against our old people's life, the way they lived, the *whey ta am* of the people, the life of the people, the spiritual life, all of the organized life structures, all of the teachings, all of the language and ceremonies.

They began to tell them, "When the people arrived, they would capsize the world as we knew it." The term for this was called *spilatch*. That meant the world was capsized and our people were told everything was evil instead of sacred. That's what they referred to, the world turning upside down. It was not physical, but it was to be the opposite—instead of loving being who you are and who you came from. It was told to the people, if you don't change your life now and become good Christians or whatever, if you don't do . . .

It's a very difficult thing for me to talk about at times, but they changed the life of the people and they began to turn the people. In this *spilatch* it was said that the people would turn their back on remembering our own village places, our own ceremonies, our language, our family trees. The prophecy said our people would begin to forget everything, because they turned their back on our old life. That was a forced attitude, a forced way to be by the missionaries that arrived.

Those prophecies in those village places were somewhere around 1400 or 1500, according to the lineage, the telling of our old people, and the *spilatch* came about around the early 1800s, when the new people began to arrive in this area, in the 1850s, 1860s, turning and capsizing the world as we once knew it. At that place where *dukwibabL* rested, the man who had that Pelican power received a prophecy power with it. That is still recognized by my family as a sacred place for these various reasons. When some people are handed down the lineal names, they also are told all that goes with it. So you have to live in accordance with the importance of that name, because it came from such a sacred place.

They began to tell, our old people used to say, everything that you see is going to be a man or a woman. We had to realize that sometimes a river can be a man or a woman. A mountain can be a man or a woman. The fog could be a man or a woman. The rise of the sun could be a man or a woman. The old people used to tell us to pay attention to that, to listen to that, to watch for that.

The old people said that in some of these places maybe a spirit might begin to talk to me from a small stream, and it might be a man or a woman, so that I had to understand—in the telling about this with our old people—and they would advise us now, how to understand these places where this man, this little stream might live, or a particular type of bear grass, or the grasses for basket makers, could be a man or a woman. These are things our old people used to say, why it's important to remember where our old people once lived.

Remember the sacredness of these places, why it is that we are taken to a place that we love and we continue to return there, to that place that we love. As we get near the end of our time, we will take something that we love, hunting or fishing or carving implements. We will take something to the place that we love and leave it there with the prayer and the hopes that I get to return there again, maybe generations later, and that maybe I will meet some of my grandchildren in that place that I love, in that place that they love.

Sm3tcoom Delbert Miller is an elder culture bearer of the Skokomish Indian Nation, in Washington state. Spiritually trained since childhood, Sm3tcoom has led a multitude of ceremonies throughout the Pacific Northwest and internationally, including in Aotearoa (New Zealand). A carver, drummer, composer of prayer songs, and oral historian, Sm3tcoom milled his own lumber to build the first "Doctor House" in his ancestral homelands in more than two hundred years. Highly regarded as a hereditary leader among Smokehouse societies in the homelands of *tuwaduq* people, the United States, and Canada, Sm3tcoom has dedicated his life to the continuation of his people's language and lifeways.

Tina Kuckkahn (she/her), JD, is a citizen of the Lac du Flambeau Tribe of Lake Superior Chippewa and a descendant of the Lac Courte Oreilles Band of Lake Superior Chippewa Indians. As the managing director for the NDN Collective Foundation, Tina helps lead a holistic, multilingual grantmaking strategy for international funding streams across Turtle Island and related island nations. Tina was the founding director of the House of Welcome Longhouse Education and Cultural Center at Evergreen State College, from 1996 until 2018, when she became Evergreen's first Vice President of Indigenous Arts, Education and Tribal Relations. Tina serves on the board of directors for Grantmakers in the Arts and on advisory councils for the Waaswaaganing Living Arts and Cultures Center and the NARF–Morning Star Sacred Places Protection Project.

1   The Indigenous terms used
    in this article derive from the
    Skokomish language, which is
    known alternatively as Twana
    or *tuwaduq*, as learned by
    Sm3tcoom from his language
    teachers, Subiyay Bruce Miller
    and other Skokomish elders.

Recovering Our Ancestors
The Piscataway Potomac Rises Again

Gabrielle Tayac

POTOMAC AS LIFE SOURCE

Remember who you are. Sharon Day explained these prayerful words to me on a sun-filled afternoon in October 2016, as a loving reminder to the Potomac River's water to heal itself and its beings from toxic contaminants and traumatic history. Sharon, a Red Lake Ojibwe M'dewin ceremonialist and community caretaker in Minneapolis, is a *Nibi* (water) Walker. She teaches that "the reason we walk is to honor the rivers and all water and to speak to the water spirits so that there will be healthy rivers, lakes, and oceans for our ancestors in the generations to come."[1] The ceremony with the Water Walkers took place at the Piscataway Moyaone burial grounds, our people's most sacred place. Along the Potomac, standing with the Piscataway people who as always for us, are diverse Indigenous Peoples who found our home in the District of Columbia area on our ancestral lands. This moment focused attention on our ongoing journey to protect, heal, and grow a precious inner spiritual core.

Sharon and the core group of Water Walkers began a four-hundred-mile journey in the West Virginia mountains, at the place where the Potomac River begins as a pure water source, which came to be known to colonists as the Fairfax Stone in 1746.[2] From the mountains, the Potomac picks up energy, crashing through rapids, eventually widening and receiving the salty tidal surges that come from Chesapeake Bay, the Mother of Waters, to embrace the Atlantic. Because the Potomac passes through Washington, DC, past colonial and later US national historic sites, it is sometimes called "our nation's river." But I

SPRING & FALL 2024   WICAZO SA REVIEW

belong to a people with an older memory of this water. We, as contemporary Piscataway people formed from the surviving tribes who merged together after the colonial catastrophe, remember other origins. When we remember who we are, it is an identity inseparable from this Potomac, our nation's river—our Piscataway Nation's river.

Piscataway translates to "where the waters blend" in a unique Algonquian language originating from Lenape roots stolen away through early colonial onslaughts. More specifically, Piscataway is located at the convergence of Piscataway Creek and the Potomac on its settler Maryland side. At our northern reaches, the Piscataway towns began below the rapids at Great Falls in contemporary Washington, DC, and Virginia. This site is why Iroquoian-speaking Peoples—Susquehannocks and Haudenosaunee—called us Ganawese, anglicized to Conoy, "the people below the rapids." The heart of our ancestral homeland directly faces Mount Vernon, which was George Washington's estate, only twenty miles south of Washington, DC. Piscataway people once lived in a chiefdom system, meaning a unified government composed of interrelated tribes who pledged loyalty to a high chief, called a *tayac*. Unlike the Haudenosaunee system, the Piscataway did not have a fully equal democracy but rather had hierarchies and ranks. There were systems of checks and balances, however, with war and peace councils along with holy people, all sectors with a balance of males and females, advising the center. Ancestors were also not as martial as the Powhatans to the south, since our affiliated tribes maintained more liberty and authority in decision making. According to oral histories first recorded in the seventeenth century, Piscataway first came into our Potomac lands thirteen generations before the Maryland Colony formed in 1632. We had split from the Nanticoke across Chesapeake Bay, following a *tayac* named Uttapoingassenem. In these southern tidal lands, we merged with people who had been living on the lands continuously for at least eleven thousand years in archaeological terms. In other words, we have created our culture in relationship with the Potomac from time immemorial—forever.[3]

In Piscataway worldview, the river is a vein of Mother Earth's blood. The water, increasingly saline as it flows toward the Chesapeake, ebbs and flows as a pulsating, breathing heart. That heart is a pathway for the Atlantic flyway, vast migrations of transnational birds and sea life; we have always embraced the global Indigenous here. Oysters, white shells, breathed and filtered our waters as lungs, also protecting land areas from storm effects. The Potomac, river of life, unwillingly transported death vectors with Spanish incursions in the late sixteenth century. Among the earliest areas colonized by the English who came to stay at Jamestown in 1607, the Chesapeake and its peoples experienced the same apocalyptic forces that waved across every inch of Turtle Island for hundreds of years.[4] To this day, in fact, these waves are still pushing into the last retreats in Amazonia.[5] Pandemics, violence, debt peonage, removals, missionization, reservation, enslavement, and effective termination all scourged our history, and all came to pass by the early eighteenth century.[6] A distinctive feature of our dispossession along the Atlantic seaboard relates to the institutionalization of race law within a slave-state context that eliminated tribal negotiations as lands were seized.[7] In the times beyond the eighteenth century, Piscataway are only continuously noted as Indians in Catholic Church records. Our ancestors were converted on July 5, 1640, and the contemporary people still go to mass at the same St. Ignatius Catholic Church in Port Tobacco, Maryland.[8]

I do not trivialize these experiences by condensing horrors into a few sentences, as there are more complete examinations in other sources. This piece, instead, focuses on the centuries-long struggle to defend and protect the sacred Potomac. Sometimes, the commitment to the sacred could mean making clandestine entry to collect medicines on white estates. At other times, it meant suing colonial authorities or mobilizing Red Power to demand justice for the dead. State-recognized yet boldly sovereign, living within increasingly urbanized spaces, the Piscataway Nation perseveres always to uphold the sacred. Due to our geography, Piscataway activists participate intensively in work with visiting Indigenous peoples coming to DC to protect their most holy sacred places. Our centuries-long work to protect sacred places, such as the Moyaone grounds, shows how Native Peoples outside federal jurisdiction, distinctly impacted by increasing urban expansion and suburbanization, persist and revitalize.

PROTECTING THE DEAD, PRAYERS OF THE LIVING

In Piscataway worldview, the living communicate with spirits, to the Creator, through ancestors buried in ceremonial protocols. When a person died in ancestral times, they were laid in a mortuary house, a *quioccasin*, and their body was prepared for return to Earth. The dead did not go into the Spirit World alone. Rather, the people waited to gather the bones until there could be a group so that they could go through final burial together. Every year, at the Feast of the Dead, this group would be buried together in a final, secondary internment. Their bones had to be in contact with the Earth, in accordance with the ways that they were sent on their journey, to maintain communication with and listen to their living family. This way, they would be at peace across worlds. While ossuary burials ceased as Catholic conventions took over, it was still essential to keep the older grounds in place. Catholicism also allowed for a degree of syncretism, and the Feast of the Dead continued with Indigenous ceremonies on

All Souls Day. In other parts of the hemisphere, Día de los Muertos merges Catholicism and Indigenous religions. Every November to this day, Piscataway people commemorate the Feast of the Dead at the burial grounds, now in Piscataway National Park. Grave robbers, some under archaeological guise, desecrated the journeys, carrying away hundreds of ancestors into institutions, where they still languish. Piscataway people have been fighting to honor and return the dead for centuries. The intertribal Indigenous Latin American diaspora and allied Peoples find solace and peace at the Moyaone burial grounds, especially when they are far from their own sacred grounds and while processing grief.

MOYAONE BURIAL GROUNDS: ANCESTORS UNDER FEDERAL JURISDICTION

I first came to understand the assault on the ancestors as a four-year-old girl, on a windy early spring day along the Potomac in 1972. We were visiting my father's family, the Piscataway side, and went to the burial grounds, also known as Moyaone. These were—and are—in Accokeek, Maryland, an unmarked ossuary now under National Park Service jurisdiction. Holding my father's hand, with my paternal uncle and grandfather, we walked up to a small concrete house. I remember a window on this structure, with metal bars. My father lifted me up and we looked inside. There, exposed on the ground, were several skeletons. Exposed, bleak bones, laid out for all to see. They were the remnants of our ancestral grounds that had been ransacked. I was terrified and started to cry. A frigid wind seemed to swirl from inside the block house. I wanted to leave. I remember my uncle saying, "This is how they treat us. This is how we are supposed to be known, that we are dead, that we have no rights." And, my uncle, Billy Tayac, said, "I can hear those bones begging us to set them free." Several years later, supported and uplifted by the American Indian Movement, my uncle and other Piscataway people tore that block house down. That act signaled a change: that we were no longer complacent, that we were not alone, and that we would work to set our ancestors free again. All of them. All Native ancestors everywhere.

A few years later, in 1978, a seminal event mobilized a deeper return to the burial grounds. My grandfather, Chief Turkey Tayac, also carrying his "Christian" name, Phillip Proctor, was an herbal doctor and early-twentieth-century advocate for revitalizing Native identity in the East. He learned that he had developed terminal leukemia. Years before, in 1961, he shook hands with then–Secretary of the Interior Stewart Udall. Piscataway sacred lands would be given over to create Piscataway National Park. The stated purpose was to protect the viewshed from Mount Vernon. Development was escalating in the rapidly suburbanizing region, and the burial grounds nearly became a sewage treatment plant. The main reason for protecting the site was not because it was a significant Native place. Rather, the action went forward to preserve a colonial gaze from George Washington's home across the river. Turkey, however, dedicated attention to the spiritual profundity of the place, where he collected plant medicines, visited with the dead who had escaped archaeological excavation, and remembered who he was. The handshake deal meant two important verbal agreements for Turkey. He would support the park's creation on the condition that his people could always freely enter their burial grounds for prayer. Turkey also arranged for his own passage to the ancestors. He asked Secretary Udall to make sure that he could be buried with the "old people," the ones who made the journey together into the early years of English invasion. Upon learning of his cancer diagnosis, Turkey made a visit to the building to see about his burial. There were no signed papers (not that signing paper ever guaranteed Native people treaty compliance); he believed that the handshake sealed the deal. He learned that day that to be buried in National Park land, he would have to get an act of Congress. When the chief died, his people refused to bury him until he could be among the ancestors. Nearly a year later, with thousands of supporters, including the National Congress of American Indians, the act passed through Congress and Turkey was able to make his journey. Even with the federal act, when the burial day came, white landowners refused to allow the hearse to go down the road. Singing the American Indian Movement anthem, mourners hand-carried the coffin to the grave, walking through sleet and rain, placing into the ground this leader who refused to let his people vanish.

Piscataway people, diverse Native visitors, and allies go to pray at Turkey's grave among the old ones to this day. To have ceremonies there, however, the tribe still has to file for permits for every one of the four annual gatherings.[9] Human remains held at the Smithsonian were not subject to legal repatriation guidelines due to the Piscataway's nonfederal status—the petition for federal recognition was first filed in 1978. The spirit, rather than the letter, of the law would be an opportunity to initiate return. Since 2007, persistent lobbying, protesting, educating, and most importantly, remembering who we are, has caused some shifts. The Accokeek Foundation, a historical and environmental organization adjacent to the burial grounds, opened its board and staff positions to create long-term relationships with Piscataway people. Piscataway tribal member Anjela Barnes is now the Accokeek Foundation's chief executive officer. Staff at the Alice Ferguson Foundation, which holds the road entrance to the burial grounds, changed the foundation's policy to open communications with Piscataway people who seek vehicular entry to the site. The burial grounds are still treated as a public park, with people walking their dogs and playing Frisbee at the same time as ceremonial prayer gatherings. There is no signage or guidance about the place's real meaning, a millennia-old Piscataway capital with thousands of ancestors lying beneath the ground, transmitting prayer for their descendants. In 2023, Piscataway lands gained support for cultural and ecological protections with a designation as part of the Southern Maryland National Heritage Area. Piscataway people are increasingly located in leadership and consultative positions with local organizations and agencies.[10] The ancestors find a way to be heard.

THE WOMAN CHIEF NANNSONAN: ANCESTORS IN NON-NATIVE PRIVATE HOLDING

The Piscataway People have undertaken a centuries-long quest to protect sacred places, especially graves. A newly revealed case, a woman chief's lawsuit, illuminates this ongoing work for justice. The Archives of Maryland Online contains digitized government documents dating back to the early seventeenth century. These documents include treaties and interactions with Piscataway chiefdom tribes. As the English language did not have standardized spelling conventions in the colonial era, multiple versions of tribal names appear. In 2009, I started randomly searching for Piscataway chiefdom tribes who had signed a 1666 treaty called the Articles of Peace and Amity. I typed in "Chaptico," one of the Piscataway-affiliated signatories, and a passage dated April 5, 1707, emerged on the screen:

> *Upon the application of Seaven Chaptico Indians on the behalf of*
> *Nannsonan their Queen Ordered that the goods which were found to*
> *have been Stolen out of the said Queens Daughters Tomb and now*
> *in the Custody of John Rose late Constable of Chaptico hundred*
> *be delivered to the Said Queen or such she shall Direct to receive the*
> *Same. And likewise Ordered that the said Indians apply to the hon-ble*
> *Kenelm Cheseldyne Esqr who will see Justice done them.*[11]

Nannsonan had never appeared in any Piscataway histories before, and nobody I asked had ever heard of her. She was a woman chief, a *weroansqua*, interpreted as a queen, suing a colonial authority for justice because her daughter's grave had been robbed. The date, 1707, was key because this was past the time when historians, anthropologists, and policymakers determined that Piscataway traditional authorities no longer existed in Maryland. The Piscataway leadership was generally recorded to have migrated out of Maryland by the 1690s. Yet, here was a woman leader, demanding rights for her daughter using a traditional protocol. Her final recorded acts were a struggle to protect beloved dead.

Nannsonan lived in Chaptico, known as Calverton Manor, and may have had the first English colonial reservation, set up in 1651 on the Wicomico River, a tributary to the Potomac.[12] The lands were set aside to bring "civility" and Christianity to survivors from the Piscataway chiefdom tribes. The reservation, originally ten thousand acres, remained a stronghold beyond the fall of the Piscataway central government.

I searched again, leading four more short passages to surface. Nannsonan began her case in 1706. It was resolved in 1712, with ten pounds being paid to the Chaptico People. By then, the queen was "quite aged" and had chosen another leader to succeed her. There were two "young princes" in line to succeed her. Nannsonan's appearances in the documentary record demonstrate clearly how Piscataway people, to their last breath, defend the sacred. This grandmother–leader's land and burial place are now on private property, as the reservation was taken over by white settlers in the decades after the case. Piscataway women, hearing about this forgotten woman leader, plan to make a pilgrimage and hold ceremony on the land, now privately held and known as Indiantown Farm.[13] We have another name to call in prayer: Nannsonan.

Piscataway sacred places, those that hold ancestors, are entirely outside of tribal jurisdiction. Entry and presence on those grounds depend entirely on the willingness of non-Native open-minded landholders, governmental agencies, foundations, or individuals. Even these small opportunities are hard-won, gained through decades of meetings, negotiations, protests, and relationship building—sometimes with the backing of a congressional representative and sometimes not. Colonial reservations with tens of thousands of acres set aside were never ceded yet were taken over. Many Piscataway families still live within the boundaries of their reservations, alongside others who originally came to Maryland voluntarily or in enslavement. Every living Piscataway has a relative buried in St. Ignatius Catholic Church, where there are still brick walls dating to the conversion time in the mid-seventeenth century. Some never have forgotten their relationship to the Potomac life sources, others find their way back from other cities and reconnect.

SPACES TO BE OURSELVES

Over the past fifty years, when land claims, repatriation efforts, and the long recognition fight have stalled or failed, the Piscataway people have moved to rekindle sacred places through our own means. In

1986, Chief Billy Redwing Tayac personally purchased 120 acres in Port Tobacco, Maryland, for two purposes: for his family home and for a new movement-based ceremonial space. He called this place Tayac Territory, a place for spiritual reawakening where American Indian Movement activists and Indigenous movement representatives from across the Americas have found haven. Chief Frank Fools Crow brought the Sun Dance ceremony to Tayac Territory in 1986, to "open a window of power to the East." Sun Dance continued at Tayac Territory for twenty years, creating deep relationships across the Native world. Movement-based relationships beginning in 1972 with Lakota and Dakota people developed into intermarriages, solidifying bonds across generations.

In a condolence letter upon Chief Tayac's death on September 6, 2021, the political prisoner Leonard Peltier wrote:

> It was always Billys intention to just bring us together
> and he knew that we would take care of the rest like long
> lost relatives coming home. He gave us connections and
> friendships that will never be broken. Those connections
> have strengthened us as indigenous peoples. . . . In the
> days when AIM was founded we did not have cell phones
> and computers. Our communications were very basic
> and we often caravanned from one part of the county to
> another. If a carload of us were separated we always knew
> there were a few phone numbers we could call to relay
> messages to our relatives wherever they might be. Tayac
> Territory was one of those places.[14]

Tayac Territory's most active years, 1986 to 2006, energized an entire generation to create free spaces for ceremony while continuing to fight for ancestral lands. Piscataway participation at the Ganienkeh takeover, when Mohawks repossessed traditional lands, was perhaps the greatest inspiration to find a place where Piscataway people could be ourselves on our own terms.[15]

There are several other Piscataway tribal places that hold sacred space for community, including lands at Cedarville, Pomfret, and Nanjemoy. Families or tribal organizations purchased these sites and have devoted their personal time to care for them. There are no full-time Piscataway cultural or tribal workers, and no state or federal funds support the upkeep of any place in Piscataway stewardship. There are also no full-time staff positions at any organizations, foundations, or agencies committed to Piscataway cultural practices or knowledge work. It is through devotion and active love that our river lands persist in our consciousness and care.

In Indigenous practices, whole ecosystems have a relational cosmos that must be in full health for fullest religious freedom. Ceremonies are not contained in structures alone and are linked directly to places. The Potomac River's health is essential to our well-being, not only in physical, medical terms, but in soulful kinship. Piscataway lands have been ransacked over the centuries, subjected to clear-cutting for tobacco cash crops, fish and oyster bed destruction, entire local species eradication, industrialization, and burgeoning development. Sustained efforts to restore the environment have made positive changes, and Indigenous cultural landscapes are increasingly considered in planning. That said, gains are always vulnerable to losses.

Climate change and toxic development press on the homeland. In the past decade, sea-level rise has observably affected the Potomac. Burial grounds, ceremonial spaces, and ancestral sites face erosion—even submergence—as the tidal river rises with the ocean.[16] Saltwater surges farther upstream, changing balances in migratory pathways and ground environments. One of the last healthy Potomac tributaries in tribal family lands, Mattawoman Creek, is subject to a county government rollback on conservation protection in order to convert the watershed into an industrial zone and make way for an airport expansion.[17] Downstream, Nanjemoy Creek, which has the largest contiguous forest in southern Maryland, considered the "lungs of DC," narrowly escaped a two-hundred-acre clear-cut project to make way for a solar farm—ironically to supply sustainable power to Georgetown University. The Piscataway concerns to safeguard spiritual space were placed at the center of these debates, a change made after years of national and international coalition building.[18] Piscataway people now have an agreement with The Nature Conservancy to incorporate cultural access and long-term protections for the Nanjemoy Forest. A Piscataway women-led organization, Nekamaco, meaning "House of the Mother," established a physical presence within the Nanjemoy Forest and waters to rematriate a healing space starting in 2019. Nekamaco is now another reactivated sacred place that creates intertribal and transnational diasporic Indigenous community. Visiting Native peoples from across the globe, from Mapuche to Sápmi to Aotearoa and beyond, touch into Piscataway sacred places to strengthen their spirits while preparing for serious policy work in Washington, DC.

Following in the footsteps of earlier generations who joined national and international movements to protect lands and gain spiritual freedom rights, this next generation of Piscataway activists joined Indigenous youth counterparts in the climate justice fight. Hosting youth delegations from Standing Rock and Line 3, and traveling to be alongside relatives in those spaces, the Piscataway future is activated to care for sacred places on the Potomac. On the riverbank, our youth and elders pray together, fight together, keep joy together. As the Potomac rises, so do the people where the waters blend.

AUTHOR BIOGRAPHY

Dr. Gabrielle Tayac (Piscataway) is a community-engaged public historian and museum curator. Gabi holds a PhD in sociology from Harvard University. She grounds her work in both living Indigenous knowledge systems and historical methods. She is currently an associate professor of public history at George Mason University. For nearly twenty years, she served as inaugural curator, historian, and educator at the Smithsonian National Museum of the American Indian. At Mason, she oversees the CoCreative History Space to train new generations of public historians in their pursuits to understand and interpret histories, near and far, ancient and modern. She is rooted in the tidewater lands of the Chesapeake Bay, caring for places along Nanjemoy Creek as a co-founder of Nekamaco, an Indigenous elder women-led nonprofit, striving always to be a good relative and ancestor.

NOTES

1 NibiWalks, "Protocols for Nibi Walks," https://www.nibiwalk.org /protocols-for-the-nibi-walks/.

2 Julie Zauzmer, "Do It for the Water: Native Americans Carry Potomac River Water on Prayerful, 400-mile Journey," *Washington Post,* October 16, 2016, https://www.washingtonpost.com /news/acts-of-faith/wp/2016/10 /16/do-it-for-the-water-native -american-women-carry-potomac -water-on-prayerful-400-mile -journey/.

3 Gabrielle Tayac, *Spirits in the River: A Report on the Piscataway People* (Washington, DC: Smithsonian National Museum of the American Indian, 1999), https://www.si.edu/object /siris_sil_915848.

4 James D. Rice, *Nature and History in the Potomac Country: From Hunter-Gatherers to the Age of Jefferson* (Baltimore, MD: Johns Hopkins University Press, 2016).

5 "A Symbol of Indigenous Genocide: 'The Man of the Hole' Dies in Brazil." Survival International, August 28, 2022, https://www.survivalinternational .org/news/13331.

6 Helen Rountree, Wayne Clark, and Kent Mountford. *John Smith's Chesapeake Voyages: 1607–1609* (Charlottesville: University of Virginia Press, 2007).

7 Helen Rountree and Rebecca Seib, *Indians of Southern Maryland* (Baltimore: Maryland Historical Society, 2014).

8 Gabrielle Tayac, "We Claim the Name: White Supremacy, Tribal Identity, and Racial Policy in the Early Twentieth-Century Chesapeake," in *IndiVisible: African–Native American Lives in the Americas,* ed. Gabrielle Tayac (Washington, DC: National Museum of the American Indian, 2009).

9 Gabrielle Tayac, "Stolen Spirits," in *American Indian Studies: An Interdisciplinary Approach to Contemporary Issues*, ed. Dane Morrisson (New York: Peter Lang, 1998).

10 "Southern Maryland National Heritage Area," US National Park Service, https://www.nps.gov /places/southern-maryland -national-heritage-area.htm #:~:text=Designated%20in%20 2023%2C%20Southern%20 Maryland,%2C%20natural %2C%20and%20cultural %20resources.

11 "Proceedings and Acts of the General Assembly, March 1707–November 1710," Archives of Maryland Online, vol. 27, p. 29, https://msa.maryland.gov/mega file/msa/speccol/sc2900/sc2908 /000001/000027/html/am27 --29.html.

12 Julia King, Suzanne Trussell, and Scott Strickland. *An Archeological Survey of Choptico Indian Town, Chaptico* (Crownsville: Maryland Historic Trust, 2014), 4–20.

13 Gabrielle Tayac, "Arise Nannsonan: Restoring the Indigenous Feminine," virtual lecture, Historic St. Mary's City, November 19, 2020. https:// www.youtube.com/watch?v =Ea6q5H_cx38.

14 Leonard Peltier to Gabrielle Tayac, Mark Tayac, Piscataway Indian Nation, and the Tayac Family, September 13, 2021.

15 "Ganienkeh—33 Years Later," Ganienkeh.net, http://www .ganienkeh.net/33years/.

16 "A River Rising," Potomac Conservancy, https://potomac .org/blog/2021/7/21/a-river-rising #:~:text=The%20Potomac%20 River%20and%20Chesapeake %20Bay%20region%20are%20 expected%20to,areas%20could %20be%20permanently%20 underwater.

17 "Smart Growth Alert: Take Action to Protect the Mattawoman Creek," Preservation Maryland, https:// www.preservationmaryland .org/smart-growth-alert-take -action-to-protect-the -mattawoman-creek/.

18 Telersiki, Noah. "Maryland Blocks Proposed Off Campus Solar Project." *The Georgetown Voice.* 30 August, 2019. https:// georgetownvoice.com/2019/08 /30/maryland-blocks-proposed -off-campus-solar-project/. Accessed April 30, 2025

Property as a Bundle of Rights
Using Legal Theory to Re-Own Relationships to Sacred Places

Brett Lee Shelton

This article draws from a common notion of property law—namely, that property is really a bundle of rights—in order to provide guidance on how Native people and Peoples can start to recover, or "re-own," their relationships to their sacred places that have slipped into "ownership" by non-Native people or governments. Native practitioners keeping relationships to sacred places as strong as can be can only be helpful in the long run, in at least two ways. First, continuing to relate to sacred places in culturally prescribed ways is, by definition, keeping culture alive. Second, continued, documented, and generally well-known use of lands supports Native Peoples' claims to those lands in court, in consideration by lawmakers like Congress, and even in the eyes of the general public. To build a widespread understanding that places are important to Native people, the general public needs to be aware that Native people use the places.

As one example, in recent years and after decades of efforts by Lakota people, the highest point in the Black Hills of South Dakota was renamed from the name of a general whose troops massacred Lakota women and children in the year the peak was named for him. The new name honors world-renowned Lakota spiritual leader Nicholas Black Elk. Black Elk is known worldwide for a famous vision for the healing of the world, and he had that vision at the peak that now bears his name. Anyone opposed to the renaming would have been hard-pressed to argue that the peak did not continue to be very important to Lakota people. In recent years, around the time of the spring equinox, an increasing number of Lakota people have been coming from near and far to hike the peak and "welcome back the thunders" in a traditional observance of the change of seasons. This open use makes clear that the Lakota practitioners still maintain their relationship with the peak. In that way, they own the relationship, and others understand that they have an important relationship to the peak.

A deeper explanation of American property law, both its history and some basic concepts, will help readers better understand how and why they might take actions to re-own their relationships to their traditional lands. I will explain first the bases of American property and the "bundle of rights" concept associated with it, then the basics of Indigenous Peoples' concepts, frequently identified as the counter position to the American conceptualization of property. That preliminary background will set the stage for a discussion of how practitioners of Indigenous cultures could use the bundle of rights concept to re-own relationships with sacred places in their homelands that may not be in their ownership according to American standards. This will provide a piecemeal framework for getting "land back," in that ownership as a relationship can be expressed and broadened prior to reacquisition of title to traditional lands. This article is intended to provide familiarity with key concepts and provoke thought, rather than to serve as a comprehensive authority on matters of property law. It is meant to present an idea, outline a framework, and discuss some possible actions Native visionaries could lead. It does not create a comprehensive list, but I hope it lights the way to discussions of actions that can be listed or added to such a list.

BORN OF THE HIERARCHY

Of course, American and other related notions of "property," in law and also merely as a concept, have long been a bane to Indigenous inhabitants of this land. An insatiable thirst for material riches provided the drive for centuries of colonization and settlement. The colonial drive to obtain naturally occurring "resources," and the land that held and produced those resources, led to cataclysmic results that are only now starting to be recognized and grudgingly admitted by the beneficiaries of the fevered rush to lay claim to as much material wealth as they could find. "Finders keepers," the essence of the Doctrine of Discovery, might describe a primary operational philosophy and approach behind the waves of settlement across the entire Western Hemisphere. The newcomers sought to gain control over as much "real" property, or land, as possible. Then, in attempts to forcibly assimilate the original inhabitants, they sought to extirpate any notions of group "ownership" and instill a hearty appreciation for the values of private property, both personal and "real."

The American concept of property grew primarily from British legal traditions, which themselves were grounded in earlier pan-European traditions. It is essentially a hierarchical system of rights, the top position of which is held by sovereigns. Operating from their superior authority, sovereigns grant rights to those below them in the hierarchy. These days, that sovereign is usually a government, but it can also be a deity. Thus, inalienable rights might be said to be granted by God.

In earlier times, of course, sovereigns might have been royalty, who many times were seen as being in a special relationship to a deity, thereby reinforcing their lofty position in the hierarchy. Once a sovereign grants rights to those at lower levels, a system is set up whereby those rights are protected from transgressions by others—especially those in relatively lower positions in the hierarchy. That is, systems are created whereby one can have their rights enforced against others, if others infringe on them. This upholds the authority of the sovereign who granted the rights in the first place—to allow rights to be interfered with would be to allow others to transgress the grant by the sovereign.

Within the US legal system with respect to real property, which is basically land and things attached permanently to land like buildings, the sovereign is the federal government. Of course, the US Constitution grounds its authority in the consent of the governed, but to what extent different sectors of "the people" in the United States have authority to control the federal government has changed over the years, and as voting rights litigation frequently reveals, there is a constant background struggle over who actually gets to participate in the government.

The general process has been that when a state is formed the US federal government passes land to that state, thus passing the rights to the land. Then, the states govern property within their borders (except that reserved from them by the US government). Thus, property is generally a state-law issue, subject to federal superior authority regarding lands the United States holds back from the states. Of course, the federal lands withheld have generally included Indian reservations and public lands containing countless sacred places.

The Bundle Coming Forth

To Native practitioners, 'bundle" frequently refers to a collection of items used ceremonially. The story of a "bundle coming forth" might explain how a ceremony came to the people who practice it, how the items required for the ceremony were brought to the people, and what responsibilities go along with the items and ceremony explained. In a sense, this article explains a new bundle, coming from another worldview, that Native practitioners may want to use to keep their ways alive as they carry on through the ongoing existence of settler colonialism all around. The roots of this bundle are in legal theory, but knowledge of the bundle and its constituents can still help Native Peoples remain in vital relationships with their ancestral lands.

Many legal scholars today describe property as a "bundle of rights" or invoke the analogy of a "bundle of sticks" with respect to something "owned." This idea that property is a bundle of rights is an analytical and descriptive concept used to describe the nature of property as interpreted by the legal system over time, rather than a normative one that sets the way things should be. The actual "should-bes" are developed and incorporated case by case over time. The bundle of rights concept is further explained as showing that property is really a set of rights (and obligations) one holds in relation to other people (and personified institutions like governments and corporations). This contrasts to viewing property as a set of rights to a thing, like a tract of land or a building. The distinction can seem abnormally abstract and almost random. Understanding the development of the concept helps to make more sense of it. The bundle of rights concept is generally recognized to have developed during the twentieth century. Prior to that, the concept was less complicated but also somewhat flawed.

The concept of property the United States originally inherited from Britain, known as "physicalism," was one of "absolute dominion: an exclusive right to possess, enjoy, and dispose of a thing."[1] The only limitation to one's freedom to use an owned thing was to not harm others in doing so. Under this notion, one could do whatever one wanted with, say, a forested homesite . . . as long as one didn't harm anyone else in the process.[2] Of course, courts were available to sort out the details of what that meant if the impact of a landowner's actions were in question. Perhaps one might be allowed to clear their lot of all trees. However, a neighbor might claim that the clear-cutting altered the surface flow of rainwater, and now great erosion was resulting on the neighboring lot. It would be up to a court to decide whether the forest-clearing neighbor was responsible for the erosion and thus liable for it in some way. Similarly, one could shoot one's gun anywhere and in whatever manner one wanted—as long as one didn't harm another person or their property in doing so.

Under the physicalist property framework, the rules that applied to ownership of a thing depended on its physical properties. For example, "real" property, meaning land and things permanently attached to it, was distinguished from "personal" property, which described movable things like furniture, money, and jewelry. Separate systems of rules govern each type of property.[3] As one example, agreements for the sale of land have to be written (this requirement was codified later), while sales of personal property normally don't require written agreements.

The usefulness of the physicalist concept of property began to erode near the end of the nineteenth century, largely due to the emergence of new sorts of property interests which physicalism wasn't well suited to sort out when disputes arose. Examples are business goodwill, trademarks, trade secrets, and shares in corporations—things that can't be seen or touched.[4] Further, the practical impact of limiting the ability to use property in a way that harmed another person was really quite important. The exceptions to the rule of an owner's theoretically unlimited freedom became the issues of real importance in the law. Legal decisions were needed when a use was said to go too far—when an owner was claimed to have harmed another person. The exceptions had effectively started to swallow the rule as far as operation and development of case law was concerned. A new conceptualization was in order.

Stanford law professor Wesley Newcomb Hohfeld laid the groundwork for that new conceptualization in his 1913 article entitled "Some Fundamental Legal Conceptions as Applied in Judicial Reasoning."[5] Hohfeld explained that ownership is not just a simple relationship between a person and a thing. Instead, "'Ownership is a complex set of legal relations in which individuals are interdependent.' 'Because ownership is relational, no person can enjoy complete freedom to use, possess, enjoy, or transfer' their assets; conflicts and interferences with rights are unavoidable. The real question in every case is how courts make the value choices about which interferences with rights should be prohibited or permitted."[6]

Hohfeld's insights were built upon by others who followed him, and the resulting new concepts about property law were incorporated into the 1936 Restatement of Property Law by the American Law Institute (ALI). The ALI publishes authoritative summaries of the law in various fields called "restatements." The 1936 Restatement of Property Law states that "the totality of rights, powers, privileges and immunities which one could have with respect to a thing are complete property in the thing."[7] Importantly, as former Vermont Supreme Court Justice Denise Johnson explained, "The Restatement made clear that one may hold less than every single interest in a thing and still be considered its owner. For example, a person who owns the totality of property interests in a piece of land and then mortgages it to a bank is still considered the owner, subject to the mortgage. The owner would still be considered the owner if, in addition to the mortgage, he has given away possession of the property by allowing his mother to live there for the rest of her life. The owner may also have given an easement or license to cross the property to their next-door neighbor. None of these parts of ownership that he has given away would deprive him of ownership because he would still have many rights left."[8]

In the early 1960s, A. M. Honoré published an essay attempting to list all of the interests (or "incidents") of ownership, all of the sticks in the bundle. As summarized by Justice Johnson, Honoré's list is as follows:

1. **The right to possess.** The right to "exclusive physical control of the thing owned. Where the thing cannot be possessed physically" because it is intangible, "possession may be understood metaphorically or simply as the right to exclude others from the use or other benefits of the thing."

2. **The right to use.** The right "to personal enjoyment and use of the thing as distinct from" the right to manage and the right to the income.

3. **The right to manage.** The right "to decide how and by whom a thing shall be used."

4. **The right to the income.** The right "to the benefits derived from foregoing personal use of a thing and allowing others to use it."

5. **The right to capital.** "The power to alienate the thing," meaning to sell or give it away, "and to consume, waste, modify, or destroy it."

6. **The right to security.** "Immunity from expropriation"; that is, the land cannot be taken from the right-holder.

7. **The power of transmissibility.** "The power to devise or bequeath the thing," meaning to give it to somebody else after your death.

8. **The absence of term.** "The indeterminate length of one's ownership rights"; that is, that ownership is not for a term of years but forever.

9. **The prohibition of harmful use.** A person's duty to refrain "from using the thing in certain ways harmful to others."

10. **Liability to execution.** Liability for having "the thing taken away for repayment of a debt."

11. **Residuary character.** "The existence of rules governing the reversion of lapsed ownership rights"; for example, who is entitled to the property if the taxes are not paid or if some other obligation of ownership is not exercised.[9]

This list of "incidents" of ownership helps makes it clearer that property can be seen as relationships between rights held by one person and correlative interests held by others. For example, if you enter a contract to pay someone to build a house on your land, and you don't pay them, in most states they will be able to obtain a mechanic's lien, which entitles them to a financial interest in your home. If you sell the home, they will get the money due them before you get any share of the proceeds. This is "liability to execution" from Honoré's list. In the example, by operation of law, a share of your home is taken away and given to the creditor as payment of your debt to them.

As previously explained, one person does not have to hold all of the interests in something in order to be considered the "owner" of that thing. Put conversely, others can hold some of the interests and one can still be considered "the" owner. This opens the door for others to relate to property, such as land, without threatening the owner's legal relationship to it.

In addition to the correlative interests of others, when one has certain interests from among the "bundle or sticks" of ownership, other interests can limit the options to do what one wants with the property. For land, this is beyond the interests that exist in other people to whom one has given or sold interests. One example of this other type of limitation is when a government imposes environmental regulations that hinder a person's full freedom to do what they want with their property. The theory in operation in this kind of situation is that the government decides that it is in the interests of everyone that owners have certain limitations. So, it's not permissible, for example, for people to simply dump hazardous waste on their land and let it soak into the ground as a means of disposal.

Besides environmental regulations, another example of how society might limit owners' ability to use their land any way they want arises from the development of civil rights law. For example, a hotel owner cannot choose not to allow certain races of people to stay in their hotel. And civil rights laws can prevent a person from discriminating against potential buyers of real estate based on their race or other characteristics.

Or course, just how far governments can limit property rights, and when they must pay owners compensation for taking aspects of ownership, have been the subject of much litigation. Justice Johnson discusses two such cases that were decided in the US Supreme Court.[10] In the first case, a developer had purchased two adjoining lots on an island within the boundaries of South Carolina. He intended to build a house on each lot, then sell the lots for a profit. Before he could build, the state passed a law that prohibited the construction, in order to protect against erosion and degradation of the island. He sued, claiming that the new legislation took away all economically valuable use of his land. The US Supreme Court eventually agreed, and he was awarded a large monetary judgment in compensation. The decision directly involved the bundle of rights and the property rules that make up the bundle in the various states, by directly holding that his interest in developing his property was an essential part of his ownership that made the rest of his ownership effectively worthless when it was taken away.[11]

The second case turned on the meaning of "public use." Landowners brought suit when a city forced them to sell their homes so that the land could be sold to a private developer. The city justified this use of eminent domain based on the hope that the private development would help alleviate the city's bad economy. The homeowners argued that selling the land to a private developer in hopes of an economic boost for the city as a whole did not constitute a "public use" and was thus not an appropriate use of eminent domain. Eventually, the US Supreme Court disagreed with the homeowners, finding that the plan was indeed a public use of the land of the (now ex) homeowners.[12] Judge Johnson points out that many commentators view this holding as threatening the very foundations of private property—Honoré's right to security or "immunity from expropriation"—the idea that the land cannot be taken away from the owner.[13]

A DIFFERENT (WORLD)VIEW FROM THOSE HERE FIRST

Hohfeld's move from a strictly physicalist view of property, whereby an "owner" has nearly unlimited rights to do as they wish with "property," to one that emphasizes correlative relationships between an owner, the thing "owned," and other people might raise the eyebrows of scholars of property theory who have experience in Indigenous thinking about how to deal with concepts such as "property" from an Indigenous framework. That's because the move toward recognition of the importance of relationship is a move toward recognition of a core tenet common in Indigenous thought.

While American law treats things as property, with roots in a hierarchical order of rights granted at the top and then trickling down, Indigenous thinking about how those things are "owned" is radically different. Ownership in such terms is not a primary or even a common conceptualization. Rather, the maintenance of relationships to places and things—defined and guided by cultural histories— is penultimate. What is important is maintaining the relationship to places and honoring the protocols and performing the duties related to those places as prescribed by cultural instructions. But internal to the Indigenous thought systems and cultures in practice, it is really all about relationships with places, other people, and other beings. For an example of an academic treatment of this issue, see David Delgado Shorter's article "Spirituality," where he argues against using "spiritual" to describe Indigenous worldviews, suggesting instead that "related" is more often a better fit.[14]

But wait! Don't practitioners of Indigenous cultures seek recognition of *rights* to perform certain practices or to use certain places? Yes, they do, but this is in response to impositions by settler-colonial property law and other systems of law that hinder their ability to practice their cultures as they did since time immemorial before the occupation of their homelands by settler colonists. That is, intervening settler-colonial systems, through imposition of property law and other legal systems, hinder practitioners of Indigenous lifeways from actions dictated to them by their cultures. So naturally, once they are educated in the offending legal systems, Native leaders sometimes push back by seeking to have those interfering settler-colonial systems establish, recognize, and enforce rights that will enable people with Indigenous ties to the area to practice their lifeway. That's called using the system to get what you need. Every bit of it can still be motivated by the drive to uphold the relationships with sacred places as required by one's cultural mandates.

Relationship doesn't stand alone in its primacy in Indigenous thought in these matters. Frequently, leading Indigenous thinkers resort to describing the interplay between relationship, respect, responsibility, and reciprocity when they are asked to reflect on matters of property. For example, Potawatomi botanist Dr. Robin Wall Kimmerer, in her writing and in speaking engagements, frequently navigates ways to help those without significant prior exposure to Indigenous thinking to begin to see how the world looks different though a more Indigenous lens. She advocates for a shift in how we all collectively see the world, so that we can learn to live better and more successfully and sustainably in it. This necessarily involves directly confronting a primary cornerstone of US property law for most of its history: the concept of absolute dominion of things in nature. Absolute dominion over anything in nature does not lead us to sustainable living—anywhere on earth, or on earth in general. Kimmerer describes reimplementation of an Indigenous worldview as how we get back on track: "Here is where our most challenging and rewarding work lies, in restoring a relationship of respect, responsibility, and reciprocity."[15]

Regarding sacred places, Native practitioners seek to reestablish or refortify their relationships to certain places because they have a cultural responsibility to do so. Their actions at those places most frequently involve performing rites (not rights!), in the spirit of reciprocity and respect, for the gifts the place offers or symbolizes. This is the sort of penultimate relationship Indigenous practitioners seek with sacred places, or seek to restore if that relationship has been hindered or prohibited. If it takes framing what they seek in terms of a right so that those in power will understand and might actually support them, so be it!

In terms of bundles, from an Indigenous perspective, a bundle of rights would necessarily also entail responsibilities that focus on relationship and likely involve reciprocity. Moreover, any "rights" would also be bundled in that those rights—in other words, bundles of relationships with responsibility, respect, and reciprocity—are held collectively. The details of these relationships are held by collective knowledge and governed by historically defined and transmitted obligations.

PICKING UP STICKS: RE-OWNING RELATIONSHIPS TO SACRED PLACES

By (1) understanding that what drives Indigenous culture practitioners to seek to reestablish their ability to access sacred places is their cultural obligations to attend to their relationship with those places, and also (2) understanding in more depth how American property law views "ownership" as comprising a collection of permissions and limitations on actions of certain sorts in relationship to a given place or thing or other people, we can then start to identify opportunities in the crossover between the two thought systems or worldviews. Owners (in the property law sense) can part with some of the sticks in their bundle without fear of losing the thing owned. Native practitioners want to use places in order to be related to those places, rather than explicitly to exercise dominion over them. The interplay between the concepts and the natural gaps between the conceptual understandings can create opportunities. That is to say, the interplay and gaps create opportunities to take actions in pursuit of relationships to sacred places that look either like ownership or at least like incidents or aspects of ownership.

The challenge is to imagine the sorts of things that Indigenous people can do to regrow their relationships to important sacred places without obtaining enough of the bundle of rights to constitute full ownership. In fact, many actions that could be described as exhibiting ownership can be performed with respect to places without actually acquiring title to—or sovereign-granted and -recognized "ownership" of—the land in which the sacred place exists. A discussion of some of the possibilities follows. The subsection titles describe various actions Indigenous people might take with respect to a particular location, and in parentheses when appropriate is the right from Honoré's list that might be said to relate to that activity. By taking the described actions, Indigenous people can reestablish or re-own their relationship(s) to the places.

Use (Right to Use)

By openly using a place, people assert a relationship to the place. When sacred places are on public lands, there are all sorts of ways to use the lands. To the extent those uses can be openly made, they can put observers on notice that Native people belong there, that they are related to the place.

WICAZO SA REVIEW   SPRING & FALL 2024

What sorts of uses might be made? Of course, Native people can take advantage of all uses generally allowed to the public. For example, hiking, hunting and fishing, camping, picnics, wherever and whenever these are allowed for the general public, they can be enjoyed by Native people. And taking part in them helps uphold a relationship to the place. Of course, ceremonies can be performed as well if they do not require actions not allowed in general. So, offerings and prayers are permissible in almost any place, whereas a ceremony requiring a significant fire might require special permitting. When Native practitioners openly perform their cultural obligations at a sacred place, the message is very clear that Native people belong there and are related to the place. For example, the wealth of prayer offerings that can usually be seen by mere casual observation on a hike at Bear Butte just north of the Black Hills leaves no question that the place is special to Native people and that Native people continue to honor their relationship to it.

Even where certain uses are not generally permitted to the public, special permits to make such uses can often be obtained from the authorities charged with managing the land or from the owner of privately held land. This might mean obtaining permission to use a place generally open to the public for a purpose that is not normally permitted, or to use a place that is normally off-limits. Either way, obtaining the permission might actually enlist officials responsible for managing the place in helping to make the special permitted use go well. I am aware from personal experience of two separate Lakota *wiwang wacipi*, or Sun Dance ceremonies, each held for a number of years on public land in the Black Hills. In each case, park management officials helped keep the ceremonies free from inadvertent disturbances by curious tourists. Specifically, they helped with locating the land to be used and sources of materials needed, as well as dissuading nonparticipant traffic from entering the general area for the duration of the ceremonies. Such was the outcome of collaboration with willing public land management officials, and all was conducted under the umbrella of a specially permitted use.

Of course, special uses don't need to be as complex as a multiday ceremony involving many people. In another example from my experience, permission of a private landowner was combined with a state land management official special permit to harvest trees (arguably more of a "Consumption–Right to Capital" issue). In this example, Native practitioners were allowed to build a sweat lodge on private farmland just outside a metropolitan area. A state land management official issued special permission to harvest, from state-owned land not too far away, the trees needed to construct the ceremonial structure. In that case, the land management official was already concerned that the trees in question would need thinning, so the special permit benefited both sides. Communication and willing partners again made the day.

Management (Right to Manage)

There is a recent trend of federal agencies allowing some degree of co-management of federal lands by tribal nations with traditionally close relations to those lands. This trend clearly squares with the "right to manage" portion of the bundle of property rights sticks. Tribal nations have seen this option as a meaningful way to revive relationships with lands from which they were removed or as a way to take a more active role in caring for lands important to them.

Of course, to those seeking the "land back"—the return to Native Peoples of wrongly taken lands—asking for co-management is asking for only half a loaf at best.[16] Further, the initial ask is only a starting point. Many co-management agreements, when finalized, could be said to contain considerably less than half a loaf.

On the other hand, and at the risk of wearing the analogy out, having some slices is better than none when you're hungry. So, co-management does represent a realistic option for obtaining some more control over important publicly held lands. It is an option whereby tribal cultural practitioners might create opportunities to redevelop their relationships more fully with sacred places contained in the co-managed lands. It also presents the possibility to care for the lands more proactively, to be able to more meaningfully uphold traditional responsibilities with respect to the sacred places.

Of course, an added benefit of co-management is that Native people are again openly seen acting in relationship to the land and, moreover, in a socially respected role of responsible management. The voluntary participation of the federal government with tribal authorities lends an air of validation of the interests of the Native practitioners in the co-managed lands. Native people appear to be more related to and in control of the lands, which validates and normalizes their continued and/or renewed presence there.

Considering co-management as an aspect of ownership leads to another possibility for Native people and Native Peoples to strengthen their connection to lands important to them. Even without explicitly co-managing particular lands, Native people with traditional ties to those lands can influence management and programming of them. They can advocate to make sure that stories of their previous and ongoing relationships to the land are told as integral parts of the narrative of each particular landholding.

As an example, Gerard Baker (Mandan-Hidatsa), the first Native American superintendent of Mount Rushmore National Memorial, initiated programming that told the story of Indigenous relationships with the land that became the monument. This opened the eyes of the visiting public, who generally thought only of the patriotic figures carved into the mountain, not the original inhabitants of the area. Now, a different story is also told. It is a story of a relationship quite different from anything represented by the men whose likenesses were carved into the mountain. Baker ensured that the story was told in a way that made clear that Native Peoples had continuing relationships with the site. The messaging even included the fact that Native people still seek to refortify their relationships with the place, even though the carving was effectively a desecration of one of the most significant sacred sites in the Black Hills and that the presidents depicted in the carving were known to be extremely hostile to Native Americans. As Baker observed, "for Indian people, (the monument) doesn't mean 'Success of America.' It means the desecration of the Black Hills; it means the losing of the Black Hills to the United States government, to white people that came in and shoved everybody out of here and put us on a reservation. So it meant a lot of negative things."[17]

Consumption (Part of the Right to Capital)

In some places, gathering of plants for foods or medicines is generally allowed. Of course, some Native people are hesitant to gather food and medicines openly in front of non-Natives, because of a history of misuse by non-Natives not willing to take on the responsibility, respect, and reciprocity required of a proper relationship to the gifts food and medicinal plants have to offer. Taking of plants outside of a proper relationship can have negative impacts on the species collected. For example, gatherers not fully understanding how to gather properly might overharvest or harvest incorrectly for their intended purpose or otherwise put undue demands on a population of a given medicinal plant, as well as possibly other inhabitants of the ecosystem.

The special situation of reserved treaty rights should also be considered in this section. The many treaties between the Indigenous nations who originally lived on this land and the United States collectively contain hundreds of provisions reserving "rights" to hunt, fish, and gather across millions of acres of land, much of which is currently under federal or state management. The US legal system considers these to be "reserved rights," in that the Native nations are conceived to have reserved them, and they are acknowledged by the "new sovereign," the US government. The rights are technically incidents of ownership retained by the tribes in the treaty agreements, and the United States honors them by calling them "rights." That's the theory, at least.

In many, if not most, cases those "reserved rights" are still viable, though the limits in many cases have been the subject of protracted litigation. When the rights might still exist, a lawsuit is not always necessary to exercise them. Sometimes, land management officials will permit a special use even more willingly if they realize there may be a treaty "right" in support of that use. Of course, more complex intervening state regulatory systems may make granting a special-use permit difficult in cases like hunting and fishing, whereas special permission for occasional or one-time gathering might be readily obtained.

Naming

Though not clearly related to any specific item on Honoré's list of aspects of property ownership, naming is an important thing people often do to things they own. This is true even for real estate. For Native visionaries, naming things makes a valuable statement. A name attributable to Indigenous inhabitants of an area asserts a cultural relationship with the area on an ongoing basis. No actual practitioners need to be present for others to see evidence of the connection between Indigenous people and the particular place—all observers need to do is see or hear the Indigenous name.

Settlers named all sorts of geographical features when they came to new areas. All too frequently, names that remain from earlier times appear to honor heroes of the past. Regrettably, that includes heroes who became exalted for actions that were not so heroic except from the settlers' perspective. For example, many mountains, towns, streets, and other features in the West are named after people who are essentially famous for killing Native Americans or after others who have similar misdeeds among their canon of "heroic" deeds. To the extent these names persist, they function as shows of force and continued assertions of dominance by settler descendants over the previous inhabitants of the area.

Of course, many Indigenous names remain in common usage for places in America as well. Those names tend to explain something about the place. Thus, they help facilitate a relationship with the place, for those who care to learn the meaning of the name. For example, Minnesota means "smoky river," named after the river of the same name, and you can probably guess the most striking feature of the river. The place-name Mankato, also in Minnesota, is a rough spelling and mispronunciation of the local Dakota people's words for blue earth. Wonder what color the local soil appears? Care to venture a guess about what plant you might find growing prominently near Mahnomen, Minnesota? A hint is that the town is named after the local Anishinabek or Ojibwe people's name for what English speakers call wild rice. The list goes on and on. I invite you to explore your local Indigenous place-names, if you are not already familiar with them, and become more connected to where you live.

In the land called Aotearoa by Māori speakers and New Zealand by English speakers (an anglicized version of a Dutch name), the norm is to put both English-speaking settler names and Māori names on signs for places. Because the Māori names are featured prominently, the invitation is open for the curious to learn what the name means, and possibly to learn stories associated with how the name came to be. Sometimes, the name might describe an important feature of the place. The invitation to learn more becomes, then, an invitation to connect a bit more to what makes the place special. In effect, relationship in a meaningful way is invited.

Simply as members of the public, Native people have standing to request that names of publicly held places be changed. One recent successful effort resulted in the former Harney Peak, the highest place in South Dakota, being renamed Black Elk Peak. William Harney was a general whose troops slaughtered Native American women and children at Black Ash Hollow in 1855. The peak was named after Harney that year. The most recent Lakota efforts to change the name started in 2014, and the mountain was officially named Black Elk Peak after a world-famous Lakota spiritual leader who had a famous vision there.[18] There are also preexisting names in Lakota (and other Indigenous languages) for the peak that reflect reasons why it is considered a major sacred place in the region. Because of the new name, visitors are enticed to learn about a famous leader and his experience there, and thus connect more deeply with the peak and local Indigenous cultures.

The first Native American US Secretary of the Interior, Deb Haaland (Pueblo of Laguna) clearly understands the importance of place-names. During her tenure, she issued two secretarial orders meant to rid the country of derogatory place-names. The first order declared "squaw" a derogatory term and ordered place-names using the term to be changed. The second created the Advisory Committee on Reconciliation in Place Names and charged it with identifying derogatory place-names and recommending corrective actions.[19]

Through such work to remove derogatory place-names and place-names honoring disreputable figures from history, Native people help make the public lands more welcoming to themselves and others. They contribute to telling the story of the land in ways that benefit all. Indigenous language names tell something meaningful about places and thus invite everyone to be a bit more connected to them. Perhaps most importantly, advocating for Native American place-names helps normalize Native American peoples' presence, validating the relationships between people and place in a very prominent and public manner. Naming, then, as an aspect of ownership, is many times still available to Native people relative to their own sacred places. Reasserting place-names reflecting local Indigenous people or cultures provides many benefits to Native Peoples, Native people, and others.

The preceding section discussed a few of the aspects of ownership that are in the bundle of rights concept commonly discussed in American property law. By taking actions inspired by that list, Native people can honor the relationships with sacred places that their cultures require of them. Through taking such actions, Native people are also acting like owners, even though their actions don't threaten the legal owners' titles to the land. Yet the actions enable Natives to re-own their relationships to their sacred places. Many of these actions can be taken on public lands with no special permission, while others can be taken on public or private land with permission from the landowner or manager. Finally, some actions, such as naming, require activism to raise awareness and build sympathetic support.

The list of actions based on aspects of ownership discussed in this article is surely not all-inclusive. I encourage you to explore what other actions might be taken that appear to parallel ownership in American law but allow Native people and Native Peoples to fortify their relationships with sacred places. More uses, more Native people acting in relationship to their sacred places, means more Indigenous presence at those places. This, in turn, causes Native people to be seen as belonging there, which is actually a step toward ownership in a much larger sense.

More use by Native people of their sacred places, more relationship, is better for Native Peoples and their survival. This is true in both the Native and the US property law senses. In the Native sense, more connection with sacred places is better because it upholds age-old relationships, respect, and responsibilities with places and the other beings in a location. From a property law sense, more interactions between Native practitioners and their sacred places is better because this means that Native peoples are claiming more of the aspects of ownership through their very actions. They are walking the talk of belonging in relationship with the land. (and showing others how to do it properly, to the extent those others are willing to learn).

Re-owning relationships in this manner can only have a cumulative beneficial effect. More Native persons' uses of (and other relationships to) places have been allowed as evidence in court cases that determine whether the land should continue to remain "Native" or "Indian" and under tribal jurisdiction.[20] The assumption in earlier times, when America thought its assimilation and annihilation policies toward Native ways of life were certain to prevail, was that eventually Native uses would die out as any remaining Native people took to assimilation. Now, this line of thinking can be turned on its head—as Native peoples continue to recover, fortify, and revitalize their cultural practices, they are restrengthening their relationships to their homelands, and thereby re-owning, re-justifying, their continued relationship to and existence/presence on those lands.

As the struggles and debates in courts, policymaking bodies, and academia continue, it is important to keep the relationships alive.[21] In this article I have discussed several ways to do that within the existing legal framework, and suggested ways to enhance and broaden those relationships while Natives continue to work to recover what was lost and keep tribal lifeways, thought systems, and worldviews alive. It is increasingly clear just how critical it is to continue actions relating to cultural places. At the same time, Indigenous Peoples are being thrust forward to show the rest of the world how to live sustainably in relationship with the world, in lieu of the colonial tendency to dominate and effectively be at war with the natural world, indiscriminately destroying it for consumptive use. As Dr. Kimmerer noted, it all starts with relationship, responsibility, respect, and reciprocity.

AUTHOR BIOGRAPHY

Brett Lee Shelton, JD (Stanford), MA (Kansas), is an Oceti Sakowin Oyate member, enrolled at Pine Ridge. He is a staff attorney at the Native American Rights Fund, where his work focuses on cultural protection and revitalization, including responsibility for the Indigenous Peacemaking Initiative, sacred places protection, and health policy work. Brett has extensive experience representing and advising tribal governments, agencies, and enterprises in a wide variety of matters, as well as contributing legal advice and litigation support for various private individuals, businesses, tribal organizations, and development initiatives. In addition to having worked as a policy analyst for the National Indian Health Board and as a grassroots organizer for international indigenous peoples in biotechnology evaluation, he has assisted domestic violence victims in civil court for a nonprofit based in his home reservation, the Pine Ridge Reservation in South Dakota and Nebraska.

NOTES

1 Denise R. Johnson, "Reflections on the Bundle of Rights," *Vermont Law Review* 32 (2007): 247–72, at 250.

2 Johnson, "Reflections," 250.

3 Johnson, "Reflections," 250.

4 Johnson, "Reflections," 250.

5 Johnson, "Reflections," 251.

6 Johnson, "Reflections, 251 (quoting Hohfeld).

7 Johnson, "Reflections," 252 (partially quoting 1936 Restatement, internal quotes and editing marks omitted).

8 Johnson, "Reflections," 252.

9 Johnson, "Reflections," 253 (quoting Honoré).

10 Johnson, "Reflections," 257–68.

11 *Lucas v. South Carolina Coast Council*, 505 U.S. 1003 (1992).

12 *Kelo v. City of New London*, 545 U.S. 469 (2005).

13 Johnson, "Reflections," 257.

14 David Delgado Shorter, "Spirituality," in *Oxford Handbook of American Indian History*, ed. Frederick E. Hoxie (Oxford: Oxford University Press, 2016), chap. 22.

15 Robin Wall Kimmerer, *Braiding Sweetgrass* (Minneapolis, MN: Milkweed Editions, 2013), 336.

16 The guest editor of this issue, Suzan Shown Harjo (Cheyenne and Hodulgee Muscogee), has repeatedly made this important point in conversations that have included me over the course of several years.

17 Gerard Baker, quoted in Indianz.com, "Native Sun News: Gerard Baker leaves behind a strong legacy," posted September 23, 2011, formerly at https://www.indianz.com/News /2011/003102.asp.

18 "From Harney to Black Elk Peak: Evolution of a Name," *Black Hills Visitor Magazine*, March 20, 2020, https://blackhillsvisitor.com/see -and-do/attractions/from-harney -to-black-elk-peak-evolution-of-a -name/#:~:text=Their%20efforts %20were%20renewed%20in,at %20the%20age%20of%20nine.

19 Secretary of the Interior, Order Nos. 3404 and 3405, November 19, 2021.

20 See, for example, *Nebraska v. Parker*, 577 U.S. 481 (2016); *City of Sherrill, N.Y., v. Oneida Indian Nation of New York*, 544 U.S. 197 (2005); *South Dakota v. Yankton Sioux Tribe*, 522 U.S. 329 (1998); *Solem v. Bartlett*, 465 U.S. 463 (1984); *Rosebud Sioux Tribe v. Kneip*, 430 U.S. 584 (1977).

21 See, for example, Kristen A. Carpenter, "A Property Rights Approach to Sacred Sites Cases: Asserting a Place for Indians as Nonowners," *UCLA Law Review* 52 (2005), 1061, https://scholar.law .colorado.edu/articles/399; Marcia Yablon, "Property Rights and Sacred Sites: Federal Regulatory Responses to American Indian Religious Claims on Public Land," *Yale Law Journal* 113 (2004), 1623–62; Myrl L. Duncan, "Reconceiving the Bundle of Sticks: Land as a Community-Based Resource, *Lewis and Clark Environmental Law Review* 32, no. 4 (2002), 773–807, https://www.jstor.org/stable /43266136; Jessica Shoemaker, "No Sticks in My Bundle: Rethinking the Indian Land Tenure Problem," *University of Kansas Law Review* 63, no. 2 (2015) 383–450, https://ssrn.com /abstract=2430922.

Returning the Heart of the People

Tina Kuckkahn

This article, which describes a compelling example of "Land Back" as experienced by a Tribal Nation in northern Wisconsin, is written in storytelling methodology, in keeping with a long history of oral tradition among Indigenous peoples of Turtle Island (North America) and beyond. There are many ways to protect sacred places, such as employing legal strategies through the court system, acts of Congress, land trusts, and outright purchase. Success often comes down to the will of determined people who persist against the odds—sometimes with what some may consider divine intervention.

THE GREAT MIGRATION

Long before the arrival of the Europeans, the Three Fires Confederacy, which consists of Ojibwe, Odawa, and Potawatomi tribal peoples, lived along the eastern seaboard of Turtle Island (colonially referred to as North America). This Confederacy of Anishinaabe Peoples acknowledged not only a historical alliance, but also roles that the three groups of distinct but related peoples carried. The Ojibwe role within the confederacy was that of the Keepers of the Faith. Many of the ancestral teachings were preserved and interpreted on birch-bark scrolls, as they are today by those who carry the spiritual and cultural knowledge through the original healing societies known as the Grand Medicine Societies, or *Midewiwin*. The Odawa, known as the Ones Who Trade, were expert negotiators, not only among the newcomer trappers and traders, but also among the Indigenous nations themselves. The *Bodéwadmi* (Potawatomi) were the Keepers of the Fire. They carried the original fire that was brought from the Eastern Doorway along the seaboard to the Great Lakes region.

This transcontinental journey was the result of the Seven Fires Prophecy, which precipitated what is known as the Great Migration of the Anishinaabe Peoples. Each of the Seven Fires foretold of an era that would come to pass. The prophecy revealed that, during the time of the First Fire, a "light-skinned race" was coming, and those who did not migrate inland were in danger of becoming subsumed by the new people. The Anishinaabe were told to begin traveling west from the East Coast, following the St. Lawrence Seaway. According to the prophecy, the sacred *Miigis* (cowrie) shell would appear at certain landmarks, guiding the people until they reached the place where "the food grows on water." *Manoomin*, or wild rice, is the sacred food that flourishes throughout the numerous waterways of the Great Lakes region.[1]

FINDING A NEW HOME

The Anishinaabe traveled to *Mooningwanekaaning-minis* (the Island of the Yellow Shafted Flicker, also known as Madeline Island). It was there that the water drums of the Grand Medicine *Midewiwin* Lodge sounded for the last time before the various bands continued their journeys, settling throughout Canada in what is now known as Quebec, Ontario, Saskatchewan, Manitoba, and Alberta. Those who traveled south settled in Michigan, Wisconsin, Minnesota, and North Dakota.

One of the Ojibwe bands was led by Kiishkiman, an *ogema* (headman) by the name of Sharpened Stone. In 1745 Kiishkiman led the group, whose federal government name is the Lac du Flambeau Band of Lake Superior Chippewa Indians, to one of the most pristine and abundant systems of fresh waterways on the planet. Located about an hour south of Gichi Gaaming (Lake Superior), the reservation was established by the Treaty of 1854. Containing 260 lakes and 71 miles of streams and wetlands, Lac du Flambeau is home to nearly one-half of all the water area within Wisconsin's Tribal Nations.[2]

The story of *Waaswaaganing*, which is our Anishinaabe word for the place we now call home, is a very beautiful oral history that describes how our band of Ojibwe first settled in the area. When they arrived from *Mooningwanekaaning-minis*, they made camp along the tranquil Bear River, in an area still known as Old Indian Village. At night they noticed what looked like a ball of fire dancing above the waters on the far side of Flambeau Lake. A group of warriors was dispatched to investigate. The warriors were surprised to find that the mysterious light was in fact a torch made out of rolled birch bark, which contained pitch that was lit to create a long-lasting source of light. A nearly blind old man was using the torchlight at night, holding it overhead while he traversed the shoreline. The torchlight was reflected in the eyes of the spawning walleye, guiding the thrust of his spear. This ingenious practice became an important means of feeding the people in our new homelands.[3] The French named the area Lac du Flambeau, or Lake of Flames. The Anishinaabeg word *Waaswaaganing* means Place of the Flaming Torch.

DISPLACEMENT

As is often the case when people migrate to new lands, there were people already living there. The Dakota people lived, and many continue to live, throughout Wisconsin and Minnesota. The Ojibwe had some distinct advantages in the battles they waged against the Dakota, including Western weaponry (guns and gunpowder), and lightweight birch-bark canoes that were easier to maneuver than the Dakotas' dugout canoes. It is also noteworthy that, during that time, the Dakota were also being attacked by settlers and the military in other areas of their territories.[4]

STRAWBERRY ISLAND

Near the center of Flambeau Lake, there is an island that is sacred to our people. *Odemin-minis*, Strawberry Island, is known as the final battleground between the Dakota and Ojibwe, a place where warriors of both nations fell in 1745 and now lie in eternal rest. The word for strawberry, *odemin*, in the Ojibwe language means "heart berry." Named for the shape of the island, Strawberry Island has become known as the Heart of the People. It is also known as the Place of the Little People, adding to its cultural and spiritual significance.

American Indians know all too well that every time the federal government establishes a new era of federal Indian policy, more often than not it results in the transfer of lands from Tribal Nations into non-Indian hands, despite the limited sovereignty established by the Supreme Court in the Marshall Trilogy.[5] One of the principal federal policies that diminished the tribal land base was the Dawes Act. Established by Congress in 1887, this assimilationist policy broke up reservations into individual allotments, leading to the loss of ninety million acres.[6]

In the early twentieth century Strawberry Island was allotted to Harold Whitefeather, a boy who died at the age of five. John Whitefeather inherited the land and sold the twenty-six-acre island for $2,105 to the Mills family in 1910. In 1976 Walter Mills, of Aspen, Colorado, planned to subdivide the island into sixteen lots for luxury vacation homes. The concept of developing the island was anathema to the Tribal People, who for centuries respected the land by not setting foot on it and by offering *asema*, or tobacco, to acknowledge the fallen warriors buried there.

Lac du Flambeau elder Mildred "Tinker" Schuman described her astonishment at the plan: "What? It will never happen!" Living on the shores of Flambeau Lake, Tinker, whose Anishinaabe name is *Migizikwe* (Eagle Woman), regularly offers her prayers to the island. As she relayed the oral history, "Tribal elders were told by their elders to not step on the place where the spirits visit out of respect to those who fell there in the war. No one should disturb it, or the human burials grounds located within it."

In 1994 the tribe sued to purchase the land from Mills. Knowing that the island was sacred to the people of Lac du Flambeau, Mills increased the price to millions of dollars, which at the time was out of reach for the tribe. Years of tense negotiations and legal struggles ensued.

Tinker was present when the Ojibwe and Dakota came together in July 1995 for the "Healing of the Nations Gathering" to protect the island. Shortly thereafter, in October 1995, the Vilas County Zoning Committee voted to deny the Mills Condominium Project a building permit, and in August 1999 the tribe rejected the plan by referendum.[7]

SPIRITUAL INTERVENTION

Lac du Flambeau elder and veteran Georgine Brown was working as a postmaster at the Bad River Band of Lake Superior Chippewa during the summer of 2013. Her father, well-known veteran George W. Brown, phoned to advise her that a great storm was approaching and she should drive back to Lac du Flambeau with caution. Georgine recalled seeing the huge black cloud forming as she made her way to her family's home on the shores of Flambeau Lake.

With the immense power of the (super)natural world, the storm broke, flattening all the trees on Strawberry Island.

"They looked like toothpicks," relayed Georgine. All the commercially harvestable trees lay broken in tangles across the land.

With the prospect of developing the island now flattened by the force of Mother Earth, Mills was ready to sell Strawberry Island back to the tribe at a far more reasonable price. Although there were some who insisted that the tribe should not have to pay for the return of the island, a settlement was reached in 2013 for the tribe to purchase the Island, ensuring that it would never be developed.[8]

A ceremony honoring the return of the Heart of the People took place on the shores of Flambeau Lake at Sand Beach in 2014. Tinker recalled that Elder Joe Rose came to offer a prayer and that "it was a smashing relief for our people." Always grateful "to our spirits that guide us," Tinker offered her prayer: "*Chi meqwech, Gitchie Manido* (Many thanks, Great Spirit) for the return of the Strawberry Island."

Tina Kuckkahn (she/her), JD, is a citizen of the Lac du Flambeau Tribe of Lake Superior Chippewa and a descendant of the Lac Courte Oreilles Band of Lake Superior Chippewa Indians. As the managing director for the NDN Collective Foundation, Tina helps lead a holistic, multilingual grantmaking strategy for international funding streams across Turtle Island and related island nations. Tina was the founding director of the House of Welcome Longhouse Education and Cultural Center at Evergreen State College, from 1996 until 2018, when she became Evergreen's first Vice President of Indigenous Arts, Education and Tribal Relations. Tina serves on the board of directors for Grantmakers in the Arts and on advisory councils for the Waaswaaganing Living Arts and Cultures Center and the NARF–Morning Star Sacred Places Protection Project.

NOTES

1 Edward Benton-Banai, *Mishomis Book: The Voice of the Ojibway*, 2nd ed. (Minneapolis: University of Minnesota Press, 2010).

2 Lac du Flambeau Tribe, "Natural Resources," https://www.ldftribe.com/water-quality.

3 The ancestors who signed the Treaty of 1854 had the foresight to protect and reserve the right to spearfish. The Chippewa Tribes' treaty-protected rights to harvest fish throughout the area that was ceded in the treaty (roughly one-third of the state of Wisconsin) became a decades-long point of controversy in the Northwoods, pitting sports fishing against tribal fishing, often with violent consequences. This led to a series of federal court cases that eventually affirmed the tribes' rights to continue to harvest fish within the treaty-ceded territory.

4 If the Pontiac leader Tecumseh had been successful in his quest to unite the Tribal Nations against the Europeans, both the history and the entire landscape of Turtle Island might look very different today.

5 The Marshall Trilogy is a set of three Supreme Court decisions in the early nineteenth century that established the canons of federal Indian Law: *Johnson v. M'Intosh*, 21 U.S. (7 Wheat.) 543 (1823); *Cherokee Nation v. Georgia*, 30 U.S. (5 Pet.) 1 (1831), and *Worcester v. Georgia*, 31 U.S. 515 (1832).

6 "The Dawes Act: Badlands National Park," National Park Service, https://www.nps.gov/articles/000/dawes-act.htm

7 Mildred "Tinker" Schuman, "Historical Site Strawberry Island," 2013; copy in the author's possession.

8 "Strawberry Island: The Heart of Lac du Flambeau," WXPR, January 23, 2019, https://www.wxpr.org/arts-life/2019-01-23/strawberry-island-the-heart-of-lac-du-flambeau.

Deloria's Invocation
The Fourth Kind of Sacred Lands

Daniel R. Wildcat

> Because there are higher spiritual powers who
> are in communication with human beings,
> there has to be a fourth category of sacred
> lands. *Human beings must always be ready to receive*
> *new revelations and at new locations.*
>
> —Vine Deloria Jr., "Sacred Lands and Religious
> Freedom" (emphasis added)

Many sacred land issues face Indigenous Peoples today, but two issues, one raised explicitly and another implicitly, in Deloria's fourth category of sacred lands are seldom discussed publicly. The first issue seems worthy of public examination: Are human beings, in this age of the Anthropocene, "ready to receive new revelations and at new locations"?[1] Deloria's prodigious scholarship makes clear that, for American Indians, he believed revelations were tied to sacred places. Place, the land, including all the life residing there, was for Deloria the web of relations through which sacred powers moved and, in exceptional cases, directly revealed themselves with special messages for a People.

Supposing the reception of a new revelation such as Deloria describes, the implicit question of whether our peoples or nations are prepared to deal with new revelations through customary protocols or traditions is worthy of consideration. In the world we now live in, not the one our ancestors used to live in, how would revelations be shared and with whom? Are tribal nations prepared to take actions to enact, realize, or fulfill a new revelation? Also, what of the land itself? What actions would be required to protect a new sacred place made manifest with the reception of a revelation?

Obviously, as Deloria realized in the last book he completed before his death, *The World We Used to Live In*, human activity has significantly changed the world we live in compared to the world our ancestors experienced even one hundred or two hundred years ago. Therefore, how we deal with what Deloria numbered the fourth kind of sacred lands, those new places where new revelations are received, must be considered. Consider what follows as an invocation, a rumination, a meditation, and an invitation offered with humility, suggesting we ask ourselves an important question: Are we, the First Peoples of this land, "ready to receive new revelations and at new locations"?

A LITTLE CONTEXT

Vine Deloria Jr. argued that any rational analysis of the sacredness of lands in Western thought must be understood as a matter of convenience: a necessary accommodation to allow discussion with those trained to think in that tradition but not a representation of "the nature of reality." Such a rational discussion at best informs the "principle of respect for the sacred."[2] How could such a discussion do otherwise?

From *God Is Red* (1973) through *The World We Used to Live In* (2006) and, some might argue, his posthumously published work *C. G. Jung and the Sioux Traditions: Dreams, Visions, Nature, and the Primitive* (2009), Deloria argued that Western thinking, indeed the Western worldview, was fundamentally at odds with American Indian worldviews. While this is true, we find interesting convergences between Indigenous knowledges and some recent thinking of Western-trained philosophers and scientists. The divergences in the way we, the First Peoples of this land, and those possessing Western-informed worldviews understand the world in which we live has fundamentally shaped the five-hundred-year-old collision of cultures we have experienced.

It is this five-century-long experience of colonialism—ongoing depredations in an institution-driven hegemonic sense—and our own more recent, two-century-long experience of US policies of enclosure, removal, relocation, and a largely economically driven diasporic movement into the interstices of the US landscape of the American dream that shape this rumination about new revelations in new places. The question I examine here is about our preparation "to receive new revelations . . . at new locations," particularly those revelations beyond the merely personal that have import to an entire people/tribe/nation. All revelations are very personal experiences. The distinction that I am calling attention to is the difference between revelations that offer instructions with consequences for an individual only versus for an entire people.

This distinction is critical, for while all revelations are a person's (experientially personal) experience, the revelatory religious experiences Deloria examined throughout his work dealt with those that had efficacy for not only the person experiencing the revelation but also a people/tribe/nation. Because Deloria postulates such experiences are fundamentally about sacred places/lands and the convergence of powers that present themselves in a revelatory manner to individuals at places long known to living tribal Peoples, the proposition that we must be prepared to receive revelations at new locations certainly extends Deloria's formulation of sacred lands.

Given our geographic movement to new places, should we expect or be open to receiving revelations at new places? As Peoples within living, not dead, religious traditions—traditions literally grounded in this world—Deloria suggests that we should expect new revelations in new locations. In *God Is Red*, Deloria argued that Western European peoples thought of the nature of the world primarily in a temporal sense, while American Indians thought of the nature of the world from a primarily spatial point of view. As he noted, neither side would understand the other if they failed to consider these conceptual differences, especially when discussing history and religion.[3]

Deloria identified the Eurocentric timeline view of history, which positioned itself as the timeline of world history, as one of the deep obstacles to an appreciation and understanding of American Indian worldviews and thinking traditions, especially Native understanding of and relationship to the land. Deloria postulated, "The fundamental difference is of great philosophical importance. American Indians hold their lands—places—as having the highest possible meaning, and all their statements are made with this reference point in mind."[4] Deloria formulated this fundamental difference as being embodied in a tension between temporal versus spatial metaphysics, which logically carried over into parallel tensions between abstraction versus experience, control versus freedom, and monotheistic anthropocentric religious traditions versus religious traditions literally grounded in oral traditions and revelatory experiences in specific locations.

This article examines three of Deloria's writings that can inform some of the questions, issues, and situations tribal nations might consider in assessing their preparedness—*as nations and communities*—to receive new revelations. Therefore, I do not offer the following as an exhaustive review of Deloria's thoughts on the topic or even of what exists in his voluminous works. Instead, I reflect on key issues that can be distilled from a small sample of Deloria's ideas on this topic. *God Is Red*, the *NARF Legal Review* article "Sacred Lands and Religious Freedom," and "Reflection and Revelation: Knowing Land, Places and Ourselves," in Deloria's *For This Land* constitute a good place to start thinking about Deloria's fourth category of sacred lands.

In the 1980s and early 1990s, the work of trying to protect existing sacred lands through legislation required framing the need and right to protection of such places in a way lawmakers could understand. Deloria framed the need to protect sacred sites (lands) by giving legislators something that would make sense to a reasonable person. He suggested four classes or types of sacred places. The first are lands made sacred as a result of events that are important in a people's history. They are typically made and declared sacred by humankind. Ironically, many of these sites are places where large numbers of humans were killed by other humans in warfare. The second and third types of sacred places are the result of sacred powers residing in those places presenting themselves. In the second type, the presence of a power not of our making is felt and made manifest in a place; such places exist across the United States in canyons, riversides, mountainsides, prairies, and so on. The third type of sacred lands "are places of overwhelming holiness where the Higher Powers, on their own initiative, have revealed Themselves to human beings."[5] These are places of revelation where specific knowledge, messages, visions, or challenges are given to the person(s) receiving them. Such places may act as "portals" to a sacred power that chooses to communicate with certain individuals who respectfully seek direct communication.

The first kind of sacred land is the easiest to gain support for special recognition, memorialization, and protection. The other two kinds of sacred lands known to American Indians, Alaska Natives, and Native Hawaiians still lack the legal protection one might expect consistent with the First Amendment of the US Constitution. However, the fourth class of sacred lands raises profound issues about our present relationship with the land and calls for a serious examination of ourselves as Indigenous Peoples.

As we Indigenous Peoples of the United States and its territories think about the protection of sacred lands, we must situate our tribal, Indigenous (that is, People of Places) discussions of sacred lands in the context of our own worldviews. Yes, we have tribal differences, and most of those have to do with the places that we call home—experiences in particular places matter. Deloria contended our tribal metaphysics are founded on the idea that *power* and (plus) *place* equals *personality* (3P).[6] This Indigenous 3P axiom represents our Indigenous cultures as resulting from a symbiotic relationship between a People and a Place. Our deeply relational metaphysics understands power as a nonhierarchical feature of reality permeating the cosmos.

The dominant society's political, economic, religious, educational, and legal institutions bring ideological baggage to our peoples and lands that is not ours to own or carry, and that we must discard and *move off the land* and off our backs. Currently, the interestingly problematic situation is that we have many non-Indigenous people who are tired of carrying this—their own—baggage, too. Before we welcome allies, partners, co-managers, or coalitions, however, the First Peoples of this land must think deeply together about sacred places/lands and our relationship to the sacred power of the land, in order to ensure we are prepared to receive new revelations at new places.

Yes, the Earth is sacred, but we do not treat all land in the same manner. Deloria warned against treating the sacred as a singular monolithic reality: "There is immense particularity in the sacred and it is not a blanket category to be applied indiscriminately."[7] These differences are a function of the particular relationship a people has with a place. Suffice it to say the nature of these relationships can take myriad forms.

The distinction between revelation and reflection is important to understand because Deloria, like many others, believes that reflection regarding the sacred is available to everyone, while revelation is rare primarily because places containing such power are rare. In addition, they represent an event where the "old categories of space and time vanish. New realities take their places and suggest dimensions of life far beyond what we are normally able to discern and understand." And there are places where "some of the medicine men and women describe their feelings as intense dread and foreboding."[8] Given Deloria's emphasis throughout his works on the unique relationship American Indians hold as a result of a prolonged relationship with the land, their homeland, the question is, How can we expect and be prepared "to receive new revelations and at new locations"?

One possible response seems particularly worthy of exploration: few Indigenous Peoples today have been able to maintain the once-vibrant, deep, and expansive relationship they had with the land before they were forced onto reservations. Given our often thousands-of-years-long relationships with places much more expansive than the reservations we were forced onto through acts of removal or enclosure, it seems reasonable that as Indigenous Peoples move over lands once well known to their ancestors—albeit manipulated and rearranged by the settlers so as to be nearly unrecognizable—the land might indeed still recognize us. Deloria's American Indian metaphysics—power and (plus) place equals personality—certainly provides the basis for understanding land acknowledgments as a two-way street.[9] It is perfectly plausible to understand not only land acknowledgments made by humans but acknowledgments of our human relationship to a particular place made by the land. I recommend serious consideration, examination, and openness to the possibility that a land acknowledgment might be issued by the land to humankind and might indeed take the form of a revelation.

Before we examine the issue of American Indians today receiving revelations of the nature I have suggested—those containing information beyond a personal nature and with import to a people or nation—I want to raise the question of how our peoples or nations would respond to such an event today. In short, supposing such a revelation were received by a tribal member, are our tribal nations prepared to deal with such a rare and important event?

THE READINESS OF OUR NATIONS

If your people, tribal nation, and those entrusted with the responsibility for consideration and handling of what Deloria called "new revelations and at new locations" are prepared to do so, then you need not read any further—stop here. However, if your tribal nation has not considered how such revelations will be handled, consider the following rumination, or meditation, on some issues that might be considered. Nothing presented here is authoritatively prescriptive, for only arrogance and stupidity would allow one to tell other Peoples how to handle their revelations. Each people/nation holds the authority to determine a proper protocol for revelations received for their tribal people/nation. Consider this one merely Yuchi's (Euchee's) meditation on issues related to the receiving of new revelations on revealed sacred lands: I hope these thoughts are useful to consider in the technosphere-blanketed world we now inhabit.

We, tribal Peoples in the United States of America, expend tremendous effort and dollars trying to protect our sacred lands. The protection and, in many cases, the rematriation (that is, Land Back), of ancient sacred places must be an ongoing task. However, amidst our changing tribal situations and landscapes—physically, socially, culturally, and especially spiritually—it seems appropriate to ask whether our tribal nations, our peoples, are prepared to receive new revelations in new places as part of our living religious traditions. As Vine Deloria Jr. often emphasized, if we restrict sacred sites, places, and lands to those that manifested themselves in ancient times, we seem to concede the point to which many lawyers, courts, scholars, and sadly, some leaders of institutionalized or organized religions seem to blindly or, dare I say, faithfully adhere: Religions are about the past. Deloria succinctly states the prevailing view of those living in a scientism-obsessed and disenchanted world: "Traditional religious practitioners should restrict their identification of sacred locations to those that were historically visited by Indians implying that, at least for federal courts, God is dead."[10] Deloria, throughout his life, argued our religious traditions, while threatened, are not dead.

Our religions are living, and this fact alone is reason to examine our readiness for new revelations. This was the thinking Deloria expressed in the *NARF Legal Review* (1991) a decade after the publication of his least-read and most ambitious intellectual undertaking, *The Metaphysics of Modern Existence* (*1979*) where he ironically suggests, "Efforts of tribal peoples to retribalize and return to their original posture to the world collapse in the face of an affluent technology that rips them apart." Hardly an endorsement of living tribal religious traditions. Indeed, in *Metaphysics* Deloria states, "We face the future immediately, and while we can be aware of the sound basis for primitive beliefs and customs, we can never return to them or take them up, expecting them to save us."[11] First, Deloria's "we" in this statement refers to everyone in the modern world. Second, while Deloria's appropriation/use of the dominant society's denomination of tribal religions as *primitive* is disconcerting, keep in mind that *Metaphysics*, more than any book he wrote up to that point, was addressed to intellectuals and scientists deeply in engaged in what Deloria calls the metaphysics of modern existence. As he addresses Western theologians, scientists, historians, and intellectuals, Deloria intentionally uses a language that will not confuse them with respect to the substantive point(s) he wants to make: an existential intellectual indictment of Western metaphysics as they are embodied in the institutions of the modern world.

Throughout *Metaphysics* Deloria is wrestling with the metaphysics of the modern world, an overwhelmingly Western-influenced world, so why bring Indigenous or tribal Peoples into this critique when he seems to be saying tribal religious realities in "a modern, electronic age . . . cannot withstand the future shock of a rapidly changing style of life"? The last pages of his discussion of "Tribal Religious Realities" in *Metaphysics* provide the answer. Based on his discussion of *oikumene*, Deloria observes "the most fruitful avenues of development today are directing us [everyone] toward a new type of social existence that parallels primitive peoples', and perhaps incorporates some of their insights or unconsciously adopts some of their techniques, but that will be fully modern and capable of providing a meaningful existence."[12]

In short, while Deloria in the late 1970s seemed doubtful that tribal religious traditions could withstand the eclipse of the natural world by what we know today as the human-created technosphere (more on this later), he was hopeful that "the movements of primitive peoples" would offer those in the institutions of modern society a chance to see and adopt ways of organizing their institutions so that they "reflected a more comprehensive and intelligent view of the world."[13] With the awakening of the modern environmental movement in the seventies and the passage of the Environmental Protection Act (1970), and the American Indian Religious Freedom Act (1978), what initially reads as a rather bleak assessment of tribal religious realities actually seems optimistic that fundamental change in religious attitudes and institutions of modern society might come. Deloria saw change coming, as the result not of a single movement, especially not one led by Indigenous Peoples, but of an emerging change influenced by a growing awareness that in 1979 there still remained peoples on the planet who understood their lives—physically, spiritually, and culturally—as inextricably related to the natural world we live in.

Deloria's deep dive into modern Western metaphysics must be reckoned with, for ultimately it shapes all of his later writing on religion, history, sovereignty, rights, self-determination, and self-governance. Even when addressing legal issues, his approach is implicitly comparative: Indigenous thinking compared to Western and/or modern thinking. His work never took the label of decolonization theory because during his lifetime, colonization was often employed in reference to a nation-state's political power. Deloria's more radical undertaking was to situate Western colonialism in its proper place—the mind, consciousness, and often unconscious acceptance of a worldview that ultimately denies community and replaces it with nearly sacrosanct ideas of *individuality*. Western colonialism separates/alienates humans from nature in a rationalized world full of resources as opposed to an Indigenous kin-centric and deeply relational ecological view of our human relationship with the balance of "nature."

The challenging ideas contained in *Metaphysics* must be addressed when considering sacred lands because, even with a sympathetic reading, Deloria's admiration for the superiority of tribal religious realities over Christian religious realities seems strangely at odds with his bleak assessment of the future of tribal religious traditions. Yet, in 1979 he saw modern institutions moving to embrace what today would be called a more holistic view of the natural world and humankind's place in nature. In the decade between *Metaphysics* and his publication of "Sacred Lands and Religious Freedom," his optimism about emerging societal change waned. Greatly disappointed in the lack of public and academic engagement with his ideas, Deloria appears to have given up hope that the deep thinkers of modern Western metaphysics and, more importantly, the leaders of modern institutions would adopt "a more comprehensive and intelligent view of the world" in line with Indigenous knowledges and wisdom.[14]

Instead of waiting for Western intellectuals and thought leaders to come around, Deloria set about developing and explicitly stating an axiom of American Indian metaphysics—the 3P axiom—essentially a deeply relational notion of the cosmos and our human place in it.[15] Both reflection and revelation are relational experiences. For Deloria, reflection on the beauty of a place and the ensuing sense of wholeness and peace are very much akin to the religious feeling that William James endorsed in *The Varieties of Religious Experience* and which Freud declared in

Civilization and Its Discontents that he had never felt or contemplated. Both reflection and revelation are a result of experience, but the revelatory experience is more dramatic, profound, personal, and consequential to the recipient. However, while the revelatory character of the *discovery* of new sacred lands is a deeply personal experience, the substantive character of an individual's revelation that has importance for a people or nation will necessarily require a process or protocol for enactment of the message or insight received.

The substantive character of a revelatory experience may not be immediately understood by the person receiving it, but if and when such an experience is understood to be transcendent of personal importance, it is necessary to have in place protocols and processes to deal with such an event. Again, I offer the following as merely a starting point for consideration.

ARE WE PREPARED?

Undoubtedly, the kinds of questions that emerge are shaped by the character of revelation itself, as a special class of experience that is impossible to predict. Given our deep spatial connection to the land over millennia and our ceremonial acknowledgment of and engagement with sacred lands, I suggest considering our preparedness as falling under several topics: community or nation(al) health and resilience; establishment of tribal protocols for recognition of revelatory experiences; and questions regarding public, private, and/or covert social engagement. This list is hardly exhaustive, but it does allow us to start asking important questions and facilitating difficult discussions about our preparedness to receive new revelations at new places.

To be clear, preparation, in the sense I use the term here, is not a checklist or check-the-box activity but a self-critical consideration undertaken with humility and respect for our histories, traditions, and cultures and a consideration of our tribal origins, cosmologies and, ultimately, as Deloria would emphasize, metaphysics.

A People's (Tribal) Health and Resilience

In *God Is Red*, Deloria observed:

> Changing the conception of religious reality from a temporal to a spatial framework involves surrendering the place of teaching and preaching as elements of religion. Rearrangement of individual behavioral patterns is incidental to the communal involvement in ceremonies and the continual renewal of community relationships with the holy places of revelation. Ethics flow from the ongoing life

of the community and are virtually indistinguishable from the tribal or communal customs. There is little dependence on the concept of progress either on an individual or community basis as a means of evaluating the impact of religious practices. Value judgments involve present community realities and not a reliance on part of future golden ages toward which the community is moving or from which the community has veered.[16]

Communal involvement, community relationships, the ongoing life of the community, and community realities—communities in place—are the environment of religious reality and revelation. Therefore, it is community or tribal health and wellness that we must think deeply about, for resilience, like revelation, is based on the physical, mental, and spiritual health of our tribal community.

The "present community realities" we face represent the challenges many of our nations might face in the handling of a revelation. The fact that many nations have within their midst many different religions across the spectrum of institutionalized Christianity poses real challenges. As ceremonial traditions continue and in some cases are revitalized, the reality of so-called religious differences, often within families, must be taken into account. Even in the best of situations—ecumenical understanding or simply agreeing to amicably disagree—it is incumbent to consider how a revelation of the nature discussed here might be handled. I have no answers, but we must imagine possible reactions among our People and how we might deal with them in a healthy and respectful manner. In precolonial times the shared experiential reality of ceremonies, customs, and habits made the kind of "religious" issues we now face in our nations unimaginable.

In our highly psychologized social realities today, the first impulse some of our people would have on being confronted with a person claiming to have had a very rare vision or revelation for their tribe would be to demand a psychiatric evaluation or detox program (given the prevalence of chemical addiction in our communities). Indeed, the historical and social interrelationships of proselytizing religions and crippling chemical dependency are real. When both are combined with the ongoing intergenerational trauma associated with Indian boarding schools, there is reason to think that even a relative telling their family of a revelatory experience might find themselves being driven to the nearest mental health clinic. Considering how nations might react to such situations is crucial.

Unless serious efforts are made to address the everyday economic, health, housing, social, and cultural/spiritual dysfunctions found in many of our nations, one wonders if our nations are prepared to respond to the reception of new sacred lands as a result of revelatory experiences. Again, those of you already attempting to address such tribal and community-threatening issues should take some solace in the fact that you are trying. And it is important to understand that there are places in North America where, looking in from the outside all one sees are the dysfunctions, but where, in fact, ancient Indigenous ceremonial traditions are strong and tribal virtues are again emerging and flowing, as Deloria suggested, "from the ongoing life of the community and . . . virtually indistinguishable from the tribal or communal customs." Also, lest anyone read the above as just another litany of the problems the poor Indians face, we must acknowledge that, sadly, the same list applies to many, not just the First Peoples, in the so-called land of the free and the home of the brave: the United States of America.

Discussions need to occur regarding customary tribal protocol or creation of new protocol for the reception of new sacred lands through revelation. Among whom, where, how, and to what end these discussions should occur are up to each tribe. Such discussions need not be public, but operating without any planning or consideration of rare events such as the one we have been discussing is a mistake. If one takes Deloria's analysis of sacred lands seriously—and I do, especially the fourth kind of sacred land—I suggest that if your nation has not thought deeply about what it means to *be ready to receive new revelations and at new locations*, then it is time to do so.

The list of considerations presented here are merely illustrative of the kinds of issues tribes might face. And we should expect issues to vary across tribal nations. But what about a more fundamental question we might consider in this age of the Anthropocene—the Age of Humankind? The planet, our Mother, has literally been blanketed in the past two hundred years with a physically heavy technosphere—roads, buildings, machinery, and the products of the industrial age—only to find herself now covered with the invisible satellite-driven electronic information and communication technology of the worldwide web. Therefore, a possibly existential question emerges: Do humans in this technology-blanketed planet still have the ability to receive the revelations certain sacred lands hold for us, especially if our "waking" hours are spent in virtual space—here, there, everywhere, and nowhere.

How Many Among Us Are Ready

In the age of alternative facts, "dog whistle" politics, viral tweets, pop culture influencers, celebrity cults of personality, propaganda, and outright lying, we have ushered in health concerns that our grandparents never could have imagined. Consequently, the health concerns raised here are not in the domain of aerobic exercise, vaccinations, diet, and physical fitness. Instead, the focus is on our mental and spiritual health in relationship to the land, in relationship to place. Deloria suggested that for American Indians the linkage between sacred lands and revelation was fundamental. It is impossible to imagine one existing without the other. When he formulated his onto-epistemological $3P$ axiom of American Indian metaphysics, he clearly captured the relational character of reality. Dare I call it the sacred and the profane: what John Mohawk called the complex Web of Life?[17]

In this context—the essential relationship of the land to Indigenous spiritual or religious experiences—we must again ask, what happens to a communal (that is, tribal) reality when people in our places increasingly spend time looking at and listening to the flat-screen realities of their so-called smart devices? What happens when the primary involvement or engagement of our people is with flat-screen experiences that are literally here, there, everywhere, and nowhere—when the satellite-enabled digital technosphere increasingly eclipses the biosphere as the source of our experiences—when we no longer directly experience the living landscapes of the places that gave us our birth and tribal identities?

Many of our peoples have experienced US government removal and relocation policies and are now spending their lives experiencing the flat-screen images of reality or, more often than not, unrealities that are produced to sell something: ideas, ideologies, conspiracies, dreams, things advertising agencies tell us we need, and of course, objects—human-made things—that tell us we have *arrived* in the conspicuous-consumption wet dream of American success. Of course, this flat-screen reality is just that: flat and mobile, here, there, everywhere, and nowhere, and that is the problem.

Deloria put tremendous stock in the power of places. The challenge we have today is, Are people who are all so intently focused on their flat screens and experiencing virtual spaces that are here, there, everywhere, and nowhere still capable of the deep relationships to the land their ancestors possessed? We even have families together but alone on their flat-screen devices—everyone looking at something different, sharing their flat-screen experiences not with their family but with an untold number of strangers.

> What happens when people are now all *alone together?*
> When their community or communities are Facebook
>   friends?
> When people share an internet space, a web address of
>   many places (lands) scattered across the globe?

These technology-enabled gatherings, literally ungrounded, take on an ephemeral, abstract, digital-space-defined character and subject-matter-defined identity, but they hardly have a personality in the sense that Deloria articulated the concept. Can we merely sub-stitute "space" for "place" in Deloria's metaphysics of power and place equal personality? I think not.

Personality, for Deloria, was the nexus of peoples and places, a particular place on the planet where the power of the land (including the air and water), plants, and animals created a community in a funda-mentally and literally grounded sense. In *God Is Red* Deloria repeatedly emphasized that events, when perceived through the lens of American Indian worldviews, are best understood as about the land, a place where events happened, rather than about when those events happened.

Deloria contended that even the creation stories of Indigenous Peoples are about places where creation happened, with little regard to a precise understanding of when they occurred. Deloria states, "Indian tribal religions could be said to consider creation as an ecosystem pres-ent in a definable place. In this distinction we have again the funda-mental problem of whether we consider the reality of our experience as capable of being described in terms of space or time—as 'what hap-pened here' or 'what happened then.'"[18]

It is not an exaggeration to say that Deloria's views, when applied to issues of tribal health or community wellness, focus on the manner in which a people relates to their land, Therefore, unburdened by making all past events and future events fit into a temporal timeline as embod-ied in Christianity's Genesis account of the beginning and the Book of Revelation's account of the End of Days, tribal religions "confront and interact with a particular land along with its life-forms. The task or role of the tribal religions is to relate the community of people to each and every facet of creation as they have experienced it."[19]

I believe Deloria understood the occurrence of revelations and their role in American Indian religions as being bound up in the com-plex relations that embody the Indian metaphysical 3P axiom. If so, one wonders whether Indigenous Peoples of the United States, entangled in the flat-screen spaces of the world wide web, still have the deep, spa-tial connection to a place required to receive revelations as our ances-tors once did. We live entangled in *virtual* room-full-of-mirrors spaces where all we see is ourselves in the technology we made. It is nearly impossible to imagine www-dot virtual spaces as providing anything more than abstract anthropocentric space for sharing information about what "we think we know" and what some think we should know.[20]

In such virtual spaces the land—an "ecosystem present in a defin-able place" with animal, bird, or reptile participation—is clearly absent from a creation event. Therefore, while a www-dot space might be a site for demonstrating feats of human intelligence and, dare I say, dis-covery in a personal reflective sense, it is unlikely to be a portal for religious revelation since there is no "there," no real place, there.

The question I believe we must ask is, Do we have healthy and well communities within our nations? Is there a *living* shared worldview where tribal values are embodied as virtues lived and demonstrated in our human relationships, our relationships with the natural world, and our respect for the sacred? According to Deloria, a tribe's relationship to the particular place they consider their homeland is the touchstone of tribal identity. Consequently, it is in the complex, manifold relationships found in the land—and for coastal and island peoples also the water—where their identity as a unique People, culture, and history emerges. And increasing numbers of people across our Mother Earth recognize our lands and waters—the places we call homelands—as sites for the assessment of community health.

We must think deeply about the current status of our relations/ relationships in these homelands or home places. Following Deloria's thinking, a good approach might be consideration of what it would entail to put ourselves in *right relations* with the land where we live today—especially if that land is a new place in a new location. There is much to consider here: Are the places where Deloria tells us we must be prepared to receive revelations located within our ancient treaty-sacrificed, unceded, and expropriated (that is, stolen) homelands, or are these places outside our ancient homelands, locations where our tribal members (individuals and families) were moved by federal urban relocation and jobs programs or where tribal members chose to move for economic opportunities? The need to consider the interrelationship of Land Back activities and sacred lands is obvious, and despite the various configurations of colonialism globally, the *common ground* we share is our profound relationship to our lands. For this reason alone, the work we undertake within our nations to remind the world that within the vast majority of Indigenous or autochthonous Peoples' worldviews land is most fundamentally understood not as a resource or real estate but as a relative and the source of our tribal identities.

FINAL THOUGHTS

I believe Indigenous voices will be the most important voices of the twenty-first century, if we are to regain a *right relationship* with our Mother, the earth. But what is a *right relationship?* I answer based on what I have observed among young Indigenous leaders and many elders— not only old people but people with a deep mindfulness of their tribal traditions and the places they call home. Putting oneself in a right relationship most fundamentally means assuming a position of humility about power and knowing, and therefore, embodying a mindfulness regarding our activities and behavior: humility expressed in a decidedly non-anthropocentric worldview. In fact, my experience with elders suggests that the notion that the world revolves around humans is anathema to most of our North American Indigenous worldviews, and this pervasive, even ubiquitous feature of modern thinking may be the most dangerous misstep humankind needs to step back from.

We may indeed look at the world through a human lens, but knowing this and understanding that seeing and sensing the world we live in involves much more than mere physical mechanics is crucial. The sense of sight is one part of human life that illustrates the power of the environment and life around us. We often experience this when we realize two individuals can look at the same image and see very different things. The different-than-human persons with whom we share the world also sense the world in ways we cannot. We may seek a correction to our anthropocentric sensing of the world with their assistance through experiencing ceremony, dreams, visions, and a mindful attentiveness to the world we share. Vine Deloria Jr. spoke of and wrote a book about *The World We Used to Live In*, with that title.[21]

Read it carefully, front to back; you will see Deloria ultimately suggests that world still exists. The fact that modern, civilized humankind cannot see it is a statement about what a great many of us have lost and what only a few still see, experience, and understand. With modern technology, humankind has certainly tried to shape the world to fit us, in a one-size-fits-all culture, but the good news is we have not changed it so much that the earth's wisdom and power have disappeared. For those willing to step outside themselves, outside the room-full-of-mirrors environments increasing numbers of humans inhabit (or are "occupied by") and leave their egos and ambitions behind, the sacred powers of Mother Earth remain ready to bestow new revelations in new places to those mindful of her and all her gifts.

Are our nations ready to receive new sacred lands through revelation? Some likely are, many may not be. In either case, if we take sacred lands seriously, it is time to prepare. How we will do this is up to each nation. If sovereignty means anything, it means a people's right to express their unalienable responsibilities to their land and the sacred powers experienced there in whatever way they see fit.

Can humans still receive the revelations the land holds for us? Yes, I think so, if we refuse to let the technosphere *occupy us*. As many of our youth immerse themselves in the new satellite-driven digital technologies and virtual imaging and realities, it remains to be seen if or how these technological landscapes might hold a sacred power for gifting revelations. My own concern is that these virtual landscapes are completely human-created, -imagined, and -reimagined. The landscapes Deloria speaks of are not, and the revelations received there owe much to the power of the physical and spiritual places we experience and which we, humankind, had nothing to do with. There are many questions and issues to be explored as some of us wrestle with the technosphere. Let us hope we can continue to think deeply about these issues.

In this fifty-first-anniversary year of the publication of Deloria's *God Is Red*, his closing words remain compelling: "Who will find peace with the lands? The future of humankind lies waiting for those who will come to understand their lives and take up their responsibilities to all living things. Who will listen to the trees, the animals and birds, the voices of the places of the land? As the long-forgotten peoples of the respective continents rise and begin to reclaim their ancient heritage, they will discover the meaning of the lands of their ancestors" (296). And, I believe, with this discovery will come a much-needed readiness to receive revelations of new sacred lands in the world we still live in.

AUTHOR BIOGRAPHY

Daniel R. Wildcat is a Yuchi member of the Muscogee Nation of Oklahoma. Wildcat is a longtime professor and researcher at Haskell Indian Nations University. Dr. Wildcat is currently the principal investigator at the Rising Voices, Changing Coasts Research Hub at Haskell. His books include *Power and Place: Indian Education In America*, with Vine Deloria Jr.; *Destroying Dogma: Vine Deloria's Legacy on Intellectual America*, with Steve Pavlik; *Red Alert: Saving the Planet with Indigenous Knowledge*; and most recently, *On Indigenuity: Learning the Lessons of Mother Earth*.

NOTES

1 Vine Deloria Jr., "Sacred Lands and Religious Freedom," *NARF Legal Review* 16, no. 2 (1991): 5.

2 Deloria, "Sacred Lands and Religious Freedom," 3.

3 Vine Deloria Jr., *God Is Red*, 3rd ed. (Golden, CO: Fulcrum 2003), chap. 4.

4 Deloria, *God Is Red*, 61.

5 Deloria, "Sacred Lands and Religious Freedom," 4.

6 Vine Deloria Jr. and Daniel Wildcat, *Power and Place: Indian Education in America* (Golden, CO: Fulcrum, 2001), 21–28.

7 Deloria, *God Is Red*, 277.

8 Vine Deloria Jr., For This Land, ed. James Treat (New York: Routledge, 1999). 254.

9 Deloria and Wildcat, *Power and Place*, 21–28.

10 Deloria and Wildcat, *Power and Place*, 21–22; quotation on p. 281.

11 Vine Deloria Jr., *The Metaphysics of Modern Existence* (New York: Harper & Row, 1979), 160.

12 Deloria, *Metaphysics*, 160.

13 Deloria, *Metaphysics*, 160, 161.

14 Deloria, *Metaphysics*, 161.

15 See Deloria and Wildcat, "Power and Place Equal Personality," chap. 3 in *Power and Place*.

16 Deloria, *God Is Red*, 67.

17 John Mohawk, "The Right of Animal Nations to Survive," *Daybreak Magazine*, Summer 1988.

18 Deloria, *God Is Red*, 77.

19 Deloria, God Is Red, 87.

20 See Alan Watts, introduction to *Nature, Man and Woman* (New York: Vintage Books, 1970), 2.

21 Vine Deloria Jr., *The World We Used to Live In: Remembering the Powers of the Medicine Men* (Golden, CO: Fulcrum, 2006).

REVIEW ESSAY *by Stephanie Lumsden*

American Indians and the American Dream: Policies, Place, and Property in Minnesota

by Kasey R. Keeler
University of Minnesota Press, 2023

In *American Indians and the American Dream* Kasey R. Keeler delves into the understudied history of suburban American Indians by analyzing the relationship between federal Indian policy and federal housing policy in Minnesota. Throughout the text Keeler reveals the settler-colonial violence of the "American dream" by analyzing census data, archival records, and Native people's stories. Keeler argues that the suburbs are still an "Indian place" despite the US occupation (p. 17). Keeler makes an important intervention in the false dichotomy of reservation/urban space as the only places that American Indians call home and adds insights into the experiences of those whom she calls "suburban Indians" (p. 6). While the text provides a useful historical context of American Indian dispossession and the development of US housing policies, it leaves me wanting a more meaningful interrogation of the colonial logics of homeownership. Keeler points to the successes of programs that increase American Indian homeownership in Minneapolis, but an increase in opportunities for homeownership for some Native people hardly alleviates the gendered and racialized social inequality essential to settler-state occupation. The access to property for some Native people maintains a violent system predicated on ongoing racialized exclusion and subjugation.

Chapter 1 orients the text by providing the historical context of Indigenous land dispossession in Minnesota during the aftermath of the US–Dakota War. Keeler describes how genocidal campaigns of Indian removal in Minnesota were soon accompanied by land grabs facilitated by the Homestead Act, the Pacific Railway Act, and the Morrill Act of 1862. Keeler argues that the Homestead Act, which promoted Native land dispossession in Minnesota and across the United States, must be considered a precursor to twentieth-century housing policies. In chapter 2 Keeler reads housing policy alongside federal Indian policies to demonstrate that American Indians were dispossessed of their homelands then excluded from homeownership by racist housing policies. Keeler begins the chapter with an analysis of the 1921 Snyder Act, arguing that the federal government should have an obligation to provide housing to American Indians as part of its federal trust responsibility established by the Snyder Act as well as prior treaties. Importantly, Keeler points out that racist federal housing policies excluded Native people and other people of color because individual rights to property and homeownership were reserved for white citizens. However, Keeler claims that, despite the efforts to exclude American Indians from homeownership in cities, they persisted and reclaimed Indian places by living in the suburbs.

In chapter 3 Keeler argues that the Relocation Program during the Termination era was a racialized housing policy that removed American Indians from their homelands and excluded them from homeownership. American Indians, among other racialized people, were excluded from housing subsidies provided to white citizens by the Federal Housing Administration and Department of Veterans Affairs, particularly the GI Bill of 1944, which boosted white property ownership. Meanwhile American Indians who qualified for the Relocation Program were subjected to invasive questionnaires and surveillance from BIA Relocation officers seeking to ensure that they were adopting American heteronormative ideals of domesticity and civilization. Chapter 3 contributes a useful analysis that brings the relationship between federal Indian policy and housing policy into clarity. However, despite her acknowledgment that housing policy in the United States is racist and enacts Indigenous land dispossession, Keeler misses an opportunity to more forcefully critique property ownership as a logic of settler colonialism. In addition, a lack of engagement with Native feminist theorizing of domesticity and its relationship to Indigenous land dispossession limits the analysis of property and citizenship that the chapter hinges on.

The Little Earth housing complex, a Native-preference housing project in Minneapolis built in 1971, is the main subject of chapter 4. In it Keeler describes how Little Earth was developed through the American Indian Movement's little-known collaboration with government agencies to address housing needs for American Indians in South Minneapolis. Keeler drives home her main argument in this chapter: American Indians were institutionally excluded from beneficial housing policies. Little Earth is upheld by Keeler as an example of how the United States could honor its trust responsibilities to American Indian peoples through similar federal housing programs for Native people. Following the Jabs family's story of buying their "forever home," in chapter 5, Keeler poses research questions about suburban Indians and argues that their access to homeownership challenges their erasure from the suburbs. The chapter concludes with the argument that the lack of housing for American Indians is a legacy of land dispossession and that the federal government could act to alleviate the need for housing for Native people who live off-reservation.

The book concludes with a brief discussion of unhoused American Indian people in the Twin Cities and some of the efforts by tribes to provide American Indian individuals with adequate shelter. However, despite the success of some housing projects, decades of police violence coupled with the uneven impacts of the 2020 Covid-19 pandemic reveal that access to public space and housing is still fraught with institutionalized colonial racial violence. The points Keeler raises in the conclusion are urgent, and the book would have benefited from a chapter dedicated to the relationship among public space, homeownership, and policing in Minneapolis following the 2020 police murder of George Floyd. Analyzing the policing of Black and Native communities in Minneapolis as a way to explicate exclusive settler property ownership would have been a welcome contribution to discussions of decolonization and abolition that are taking place in Native American and Indigenous studies. This book will be useful to those in public policy who may be unfamiliar with federal Indian policy.

AUTHOR BIOGRAPHY

Stephanie Lumsden (she/her) is a member of the Hoopa Valley Tribe. Her research examines the relationship between Indigenous dispossession and the development of the carceral settler state in northwestern California. Stephanie is currently a University of California Presidential Postdoctoral Fellow in the History Department at UC Santa Cruz. In fall 2025, Stephanie will be joining the Native American Studies Department at UC Davis as an assistant professor.

Our Fire Survives the Storm
A Cherokee Literary History, Citizenship and Sovereignty Edition
Daniel Heath Justice

"With clarity of voice and vision, Daniel Heath Justice models the wisdom that comes from reflection, the importance of returning to intellectual roots, and the compassion to look unflinchingly at how Cherokee scholarship is ever-evolving, responsive, awake, and burning. This book is a revelation."
—**Jodi A. Byrd** (Chickasaw), author of *Indigenomicon*

$25.95 paperback | 384 pages | Dec. 2025 | Indigenous Americas Series

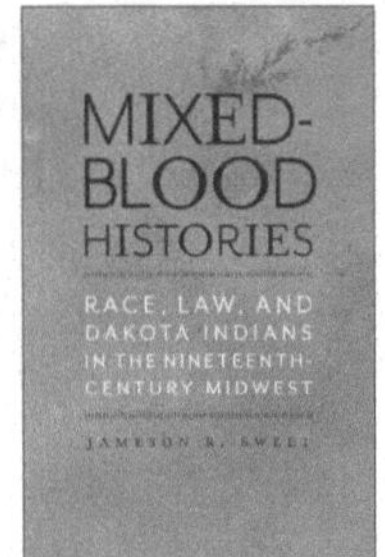

First Light
Kanaka ʻŌiwi Resistance to Settler Science at Mauna a Wākea
Iokepa Casumbal-Salazar

"Masterfully situates the conflict within a constellation of colonial violences: settler colonialism, capitalism, big science, and militarism." —**Jamaica Heolimeleikelani Osorio**, author of *Remembering Our Intimacies*

$30.00 paperback | 336 pages | Nov. 2025

By Their Work
Indigenous Women's Digital Media in North America
Joanna Hearne and Karrmen Crey, editors

A first-of-its-kind collection to transform our understanding of digital media from **Indigenous women creators**

$30.00 paperback | 344 pages | Nov. 2025

Indigenous Inhumanities
California Indian Studies after the Apocalypse
Mark Minch-de Leon

"A mind-blowing framework that informs Indigenous story in ways we don't yet recognize." —**Deborah A. Miranda**, author of *Bad Indians*

$30.00 paperback | 352 pages | Nov. 2025
Indigenous Americas Series

Mixed-Blood Histories
Race, Law, and Dakota Indians in the Nineteenth-Century Midwest
Jameson R. Sweet

"Equally impressive and innovative, *Mixed-Blood Histories* fills the historiographic need for studies on mixed-ancestry Dakota men and women." —**Linda M. Clemmons**, author of *Unrepentant Dakota Woman*

$30.00 paperback | 352 pages | Nov. 2025